ABSTRACTION CLUSTERS TO UNDERSTAND DIGITAL DEVELOPMENT: INTRODUCING THE SETA MODEL

Beatrice Bonami

ABSTRACTION CLUSTERS TO UNDERSTAND DIGITAL DEVELOPMENT: INTRODUCING THE SETA MODEL

Bibliografische Information der Deutschen Nationalbibliothek
Die Deutsche Nationalbibliothek verzeichnet diese Publikation in der
Deutschen Nationalbibliografie, detaillierte bibliografische Daten sind im
Internet über http://dnb.d-nb.de abrufbar.

Die Online-Version dieser Publikation ist auf dem Repositorium der
Universität Tübingen frei verfügbar (Open Access).
http://hdl.handle.net/10900/131452
http://nbn-resolving.de/urn:nbn:de:bsz:21-dspace-1314527
http://dx.doi.org/10.15496/publikation-72810

Tübingen Library Publishing 2022
Universitätsbibliothek Tübingen
Wilhelmstraße 32
72074 Tübingen
druckdienste@ub.uni-tuebingen.de
https://tlp.uni-tuebingen.de

ISBN (Paperback): 978-3-946552-66-6
ISBN (PDF): 978-3-946552-67-3

Umschlaggestaltung: Sandra Binder, Universität Tübingen
Coverabbildung: Beatrice Bonami
Satz: Beatrice Bonami
Druck und Bindung: Open Publishing GmbH
Printed in Germany

Table of Figures

Table of Abbreviations

AI – Artificial Intelligence
ANT – Actor-Network Theory
COVID-19 – Corona Virus Disease 2019
DEM – Deep Ecology Movement
ERIC – Educational Resources Information Center
GIS – Geographic Information Systems
OECD – Organization for Economic Co-operation and Development
ICT – Information and Communication Technologies
IoT – Internet of Things
IoV – Internet of Values
ITU – International Telecommunication Union
PDU – Protocol Data Unit
PRISMA – Preferred Reporting Items for Systematic Reviews and Meta-Analyses
SAP – Service Access Point
SETA – Social Technical Model for Education Technology Application
STS – Science Technology and Society
UCL – University College London

Table of Content

Abstract

This work investigates the interface between the epistemological field of education, human development, and digital technologies. Grounded on complexity, actor-network theory, action ecology, and hybridism, the central hypothesis is that an excessively technical conception about the mentioned interface can disadvantage the debate on educational technologies, treating them only as a tool or a means to an end. This research proposes ten theoretical categories for understanding digital applications, when considering that digital technologies expand human skills' horizons. Three abstraction clusters (instrument, power, and actant network) derive from the ten categories, and compose the SETA model, an evaluative framework to understand educational technologies and possible applications. This book results from doctoral thesis research and presents the SETA model and its methodological considerations.

Keywords: education, digital technology development, instrument, power, actant networks, social-technical model, innovation.

Acknowledgments

I want to acknowledge the full support received by the Internationales Zentrum für Ethik in den Wissenschaften (IZEW) and the program Teach@Tübingen, both at Universität Tübingen. I would also like to thank colleagues who have supported me in developing my research, namely my kind Director Prof. Dr. Regina Ammicht-Quinn, and Dr. Cordula Brand, who believed in my work and offered me the possibility to publish it.

I would also like to acknowledge and thank the institutions that welcomed my work during the Doctoral Degree (Universidade de São Paulo/Brazil, University College London/UK and the Universitá degli Studi di Roma/Italy) and my supervisors: Prof. Dr. Brasilina Passarelli, Prof. Dr. Selena Nemorin and Prof. Dr. Mariella Nocenzi. Thank you for everything.

Prologue

Reflections on Knowledge Development

Beatrice Bonami

Discussions about the study of methodological procedures highlight the relevance between deduction (inspired by Socrates' logic based on the prominence of logical reasoning) and induction methods (guided by Renee Descartes based on empiricism). While Deduction, through logical reasoning, tended to specific answers, Induction, through empiricism, tended towards universality (research on a sample would serve as an illustration of an entire population).

Karl Popper discusses methods of a possible theory of knowledge using an optimistic perspective (making the world's knowledge feasible), a pessimistic one (denying knowledge to humankind), and a skeptical one (not evidencing the truth). Popper's analysis prioritizes the study of Immanuel Kant's work and his principles about reason and logic (specifically in his argument about immanent and transcendent criticism). This theoretical foundation serves him to narrate the methodological ups and downs present in the human journey in searching for knowledge.

The theory of knowledge is what Popper calls the 'science of science' and would therefore be a theoretical science that also contains free stipulations (for example, definitions) that do not consist, however, only in conventions but in statements that are refutable through comparison with the methods. According to the assessment of deduction (logical deduction) and induction's (generalization) importance, theories of knowledge can have a deductivist or inductivist orientation. Classical rationalism (Descartes, Spinoza), for example, has a strict deductivist orientation (its model is geometric deduction [Euclidian]); classical empiricism, on the contrary, has an inductive orientation.

At the beginning of his work, Popper defines two fundamental problems of the Theory of Knowledge: the human problem of induction and the conceptual problem of demarcation. He establishes that his attention will turn more significantly to the demarcation problem.

Popper argues that the Theory of Knowledge is supported by a deductivist logic, arguing that the rejection of induction leads to the hypothetism (which he calls a set of preliminary assumptions and unjustified anticipations or conjectures) that leads to a reduction from universal factual statements to particular empirical propositions. His analysis of reason and logic is based on the Kantian criteria of purely logical distinction: a priori (analytical judgment) and a posteriori (synthetic review). Analytical conclusions are tautological about their principle of "non-contradiction," whereas synthetic determination depends on the fact that there can be no decision about truth or falsehood, just by logic.

Popper introduces the approximate character of knowledge about reality, leaving two gaps to be filled: uncertainty and optimism. The principle of uncertainty exercised by relativist thinking attributes to the observation of phenomena the responsibility of narrating a portion of the truth, giving space to facts and contradictions that may emerge from the continuity of this analysis.

This continuity can be expressed by optimism in the human power of unveiling probabilities, which he will call the approximate character of knowledge. The gap between uncertainty and optimism makes room for probabilistic positions, which Popper analyzes under the argument that the parts of simple propositions are no longer satisfactory for two reasons: strict positivism is logically valid. Still, it does not apply to the theory of knowledge—for not explaining the existence of laws of nature. Apriorism gives excessive proof since it can prove their existence but not explain the reason for their existence. This discussion includes probabilistic positions that agree with positivism and recognize apriorism.

Popper shifts his argument from induction to address the problem of demarcation (which, according to the author, is the most demanding of attention) based on studies of probability and uncertainty. To begin the narrative around demarcation, he relies on both Kant (in his limit to knowledge) and Wittgenstein (in his limit to thought) to direct his critique of the concept of meaning, in which he states that the criticism of the idea of meaning is not only conclusive critique of pseudo propositional positions but of the problem of induction in general.

According to Popper, the demarcation problem appears in Wittgenstein as a primordial task of philosophy: philosophy limits the disputed territory of natural science. It must delimit the thinkable and, with that, the unthinkable. The realm of the thinkable, of the meaningful, is the realm of propositions that represent the existence and non-existence of states of affairs (that is, the kingdom of definitively verifiable particular factual statements); it is the territory of natural science.

Breaking barriers or (in Popper's terminology) demarcation would expand the limit beyond the concept of meaning, where the unthinkable and nonsense are still in the realm of what is probable. According to him, philosophy is not dedicated to explaining, only to limiting, thus being the actual demarcation activity, protecting the territory of meaning and separating its domains (the Natural and the Social).

After his study, Popper proposes a solution (since his first action is to establish a problem) in the form of conceptual definitions and propositions derived from them. However, he acknowledges that his work is not free from contradictions, which appears to be a natural situation in science. The author then states that there is no permanent solution, contrary to a problem's expected. The definitions (because they have multiple and probabilistic propositions) will sometimes confluence and sometimes conflict with the philosophical arguments of a particular space/time.

In other words, attributing definitions, predictions, procedures, concepts analysis, and knowledge value will be factors liable to congruence and inconsistency while alive within the scientific discussion. According to Popper, the very idea of theory (a system of implicit conceptual and empirical definitions) depends on this activity, as if the philosophical/scientific argument behaved like a living autonomous organism (or self-eco-organized as proposed by Edgar Morin).

Popper reaffirms his preference in naming his work as a "General Theory of Methods" and not "Methodology." The critical consequence of methodological applications is more interesting than the methods' simple use and study. He ends his work by stating that there is only one fundamental problem in the Theory of Knowledge—demarcation—as the problem of induction arises from the demarcation itself.

So the issue of demarcation seems to be the only fundamental problem of the theory of knowledge in general (this was recognized as clearly as possible by Wittgenstein). In other words: a correct view of knowledge, which can avoid controversial deviations, does not need to get involved with the situation of the historical-dialectical problem; the problem of induction and the concept of induction would not need to figure in it because there is no induction in the sense of the theory of knowledge.

Popper understands the limitation of human observation concerning mundane phenomena and the incoherence of empirical sciences in formulating universal theories (since the methods of apprehension are limited). Part of his analysis is dedicated to understanding the arrogance of anthropocentrism and the human tendency to judge oneself capable of predicting and responding to these phenomena. Still, he questions the divorce between empiricism and metaphysics, the former originating from the latter.

Based on this, Popper adds a clause about the falsifiability of science: the possibility that a hypothesis is false or wrong. The principle of falsifiability emerges from the scientific limitation (in dialogue with the human problem of induction). It recognizes that the hypotheses, contrary to popular belief, are confirmed through their exercise of refutation. He explains that when a premise is established, for it to claim to be scientific, it is exposed to tests and trials or, in other words, attempts to refute it. If these exercises prove fruitless, the hypothesis is confirmed.

The possibility of a theory being refuted constituted the very essence of scientific nature for the philosopher. Thus, a theory can only be considered scientific when it is falsifiable; that is when it is possible to prove it false. The movement around its falsifiability is justified by scientific progress: something that is proven leaves no room for doubt and dies in the eyes of science since they no longer dedicate themselves to investigating it. The works of Thomas Khun (2013) and Bruno Latour (1987) in his work "Science in Action" start from this principle and describe the movements around scientific proof and the veiled communication between the different areas of knowledge.

Falsability Principle and Scientific Paradigms

Thomas Khun dedicates his work to understand how the main revolutions in the history of science were structured to identify patterns and repetitions between such events. His objective is to outline a concept of science that emerges from these records, warning that science does not develop through the accumulation of discoveries, as they do not happen linearly with the arrow of time (concept to be explored in Gell-Mann, 1995).

Kuhn calls "normal science" research based on one or more past scientific achievements, guided by the adoption or rupture of "paradigms" of scientific groups. To talk about paradigms, it is necessary to clarify that they apply a cohort of notions or rules by a group or a scientific community since there are no universal paradigms (Popper's criticism of the problem of induction). Kuhn defines a paradigm as a set of rules and standards accepted by a group or scientific community. The meaning of "model" and "standard" connects to an established point of view or previous conception.

Paradigms will work to allow the reproduction of examples, preparing experiments to find solutions and, therefore, being successful. However, being successful means neither being successful with a single problem nor being remarkably successful with a large number. At first, the success of a paradigm is essentially a promise that can discover in selected and still incomplete examples. Normal science consists of updating this promise, an update obtained by expanding the knowledge of the facts that the paradigm presents as particularly relevant.

The paradigm is a piece of a puzzle, the puzzle being defined here as its everyday joints: a game/problem that tests the ingenuity of the human mind. However, a clause not present in its daily use resembles Popper's principle of falsifiability: a good problem has a solution, but not definitive or irrevocable. Normal science is dedicated to solving puzzles, giving the solver maturity and experience in the non-definitive resolution of issues, being an activity determined by rules (scientists stand as reproducers or inspectors for applying these rules).

However, the nature of the paradigm lies in the identification that either the rules are incorrect or insufficient, which leads to a paradigm shift to operate on other dogmas to be elaborated since, according to Kuhn, rules derive from paradigms. Still, paradigms can direct research even in the absence of rules. Kuhn runs through the second half of his work, analyzing the dynamic movement between some of the assumptions established in the first half. By reporting cases of scientific discoveries, primarily in physics and chemistry, the author shows the concept of induced discovery and anomaly. According to him, the perception of the anomaly (a phenomenon not prepared or predicted by the paradigm) plays a crucial role in questioning his analysis patterns.

When observing an anomaly, the first questions are not in the paradigm sphere. Still, the errors the researcher may make (failures in instrumentation, measurements, laboratory conditions, or the interpretations themselves). Understanding that the anomaly does not come from committed failures but a possible hole in the established standards for data interpretation, it is considered a paradigm shift, resulting in a change in procedures and expectations.

However, Kuhn warns that the discovery is induced by pre-established paradigms and is predicted by the falsifiability principle itself: the anomaly is visible only against the background provided by the paradigm. In other words, while discussions about scientific functionality circle around the success of proof (Eureka!), the becoming of science moves a parallel spiral toward refutation. There is, therefore, an abyss between the scientist's expectation and progress, moved and articulated by the constant renewal of paradigms: science is an activity in crisis.

Karl Popper, Thomas Kuhn, and Murray Gell-Mann relied on the story of Albert Einstein and his repeal of Newtonian Theory, which operated as a solid paradigm since its initial propositions. A crisis is a necessary precondition for the emergence of new theories. This already suggests that an examination of a rejection of a paradigm will reveal more clearly and more fully: a scientific approach, having attained paradigm status, is only considered invalid when an alternative is available to replace it.

The paradigm break, resolution, or transition is not a cumulative phenomenon. Furthermore, a set of observed qualities reveals a new face of truth, even being noticed with the same lens as before. Naturally, the first reaction is the refutation and repetition of processes that lead to the exclusion of this warned new quality. The new paradigm suddenly emerges, not in the scope of the experiment but in the researcher's mind, and this event is called the scientific revolution.

Kuhn explains that scientific revolutions are non-cumulative developmental episodes in which an obsolete paradigm undergoes a replacement (the revolution is the exact moment of this transition). The author proposes a way for this observation of the anomaly to take as a foundation to walk smoothly towards the paradigmatic change: the set of information about a given phenomenon provides a map whose details are elucidated by mature scientific research.

By learning a paradigm, the scientist acquires at the same time a theory, methods, and scientific standards that usually make up an inexplicable mixture, therefore justifying the necessity of drawing a map of involved entities in this process so that scientists can guide themselves into theoretical puzzles. This map of details elucidated by mature scientific research would be an examination of the interactions between the actants operating in the scientific revolution. Kuhn states that this map is a methodological procedure naturally developed by scientists in confusion with their fields of knowledge patterns. Is a need to organize concepts, samples, criteria, and objectives to trace a viable path to the delivery of research since the data itself is not stable.

In short, a paradigm is dedicated to governing a group of practitioners and not an object of research. Kuhn conveys the concept of paradigm in two different senses: a set of standards, rules, and beliefs; and a concrete solution of puzzles that may (or may not) replace explicit rules as a basis for solving other games/problems. In both senses, the paradigm is the element shared by a scientific community, leading its operations according to its predictions, calling into question a system of results and expectations on the part of the scientists involved in its proof and reproduction (with a focus on successor researchers). By these variables, Kuhn situates the scientific practice as esoteric, dependent on puzzle-solving answers and a system of mystiques surrounding paradigmatic existence.

Ecology of Action in Science

The topic of deterministic separation between the areas of knowledge in science is addressed by authors who, throughout the 20th century, dedicated themselves to investigating the dissolution of epistemological barriers to stipulate an end to at least one of the fundamental problems of the Theory of Knowledge. Under this agenda, it is possible to explore the work of Bruno Latour. He dedicated himself to questioning the roots of the word "Social" and why science separates Social and Natural as opposite poles of reasoning and investigation.

Latour (1993) begins his study by questioning the question of modernity and, through his famous phrase "We were never modern," he warns that even though the arrow of time progresses in its overwhelming force, the human sphere is still detained to conservative behaviors and demarcations, and that would be why one is never modern even if inhabiting post-modernity. According to the author, modernity came to break down subject barriers and to claim other faculties of thought that questioned knowledge as a classic logical exercise.

Latour draws an analysis between the works of Robert Boyle (the so-called founder of chemical science) and Thomas Hobbes (founder of political science) to demonstrate that the separations between Social and Natural sciences are fruitless. He explains that the method of observation/attention to natural phenomena as a lens of truth is not enough, as these phenomena themselves lacked their reproduction in an inert space (the laboratory) to be analyzed far from natural variables, that is: even natural phenomena are manufactured artificially as the social ones.

This argument is extended to the political sciences, where Latour argues that man's situation in society and its propositions (in the form of treaties and constitutions) are also artificial. They are anthropocentric creation that tries to ensure the domain of the truth. Latour then puts forward the concept of "matter of fact" and his attempt to understand what is concretely known about the composition of truth since what humans are dedicated to observing is manufactured (either in nature or in society).

Near Popper's demarcation problem, Latour draws the Social Pole and Natural Pole as the heritage of modernity and describes the Postmodern Era's attempts to break through these barriers. He explores that modernity establishes four tasks to solve the so-called demarcation problem: purification, translation, mediation, and proliferation. In an environment where there are humans [approached by Social Sciences] and non-humans [approached by Natural Sciences] objects, this separation between the poles is called "purification."

When there are transdisciplinary fields, the purification doesn't work [for the interdisciplinary character of research objects], and that's when the translation and mediation of objects happen so that multiple science fields can study them. Insofar these processes occur, research objects become a hybrid between both Social and Natural poles not pertaining to either of them and staying in the middle. Latour, however, explains that the precise task of modernity is to try to purify those objects so they can be put back in their respective poles.

Yet, while modernity is concerned with purifying scientific objects, the almost-non-human or almost-human objects proliferate, making proliferation the most vital task. However, modernity tries to fight its existence. To sum up: these four works concern the judgment of the study object's essence in each subject area. He explains that things that could not be from the social or natural pole during the purification process have characteristics that sometimes fit into one pole and sometimes into another.

This led to the formulation of the category of hybrids, which could not be included in either of the poles as they fit into two natures. While modernity was duly occupied with the service of purifying essences, the proliferation of hybrids, which paved the way for post-modernity, went unnoticed. Hybrids are entities that can neither be characterized as humans (originating from the Social Pole) or objects/non-humans (stemming from the Natural Pole). With their proliferation, the purification work became impassible (as a matter of high quantitative), and the judgment of their actions was preferable to their essence.

From this, Latour (1999) defined everything as an actor (or actant) that acts and formulated the Actor-Network Theory. Later, inspired by the literary structure of Thomas Kuhn's work, Latour conceived his work "Science in Action" with a focus on the narrative of scientific revolutions, establishing the different actants involved in the construction of a scientific fact. Latour laments the general lack of interest in the construction of science, claiming that researchers and other interested parties are too committed to defending scientific fact, leaving little time to study it. However, he recognizes the importance of the study of methodological procedures, claiming that only through methodological rules is it possible to understand the advent of science (a rule here in his correspondence to Kuhn's patterns).

In "Science in Action," Latour (1987) claims that when he gets closer to the places where facts and machines are created, he enters the midst of controversies. Controversy is the place and time of action observation (like observing an H2O particle at room temperature; the controversy would be the point of its movement at 100°C). In general, controversies emerge from what Latour (1999) calls Black Boxes: when controversies are silenced, they are inside a Black Box, and to observe them, it is necessary to open the box (a direct reference to the myth of Pandora's Box).

Latour (1999) warns about a categorical definition of the expression black box and sums it up to assert that the congregation of disordered and unreliable allies is slowly transformed into something very similar to an organizing whole. When such cohesion is achieved, that's when a black box is formed. In his work, Latour observes controversies in some scientific experiments in the biological sciences, among other branches of postmodern science, and proceeds to report the actants involved in academic research: support foundations, researchers, advisors, related literature, instruments, laboratories, coffee breaks, scientific articles, among others.

According to him, the construction of the fact is an instrument that takes the researchers from the article to what supports the report, from the many resources mobilized in the text to the many more resources mobilized to create the visual displays of the texts and it's foremost a collective and complex activity. According to Latour, a person/human/researcher alone only constructs dreams, opinions, and emotions, not facts.

The question of complexity within the controversy does not depend on its technical or scientific level but on the number of associations it can draw. The concept of complexity worked out by Latour is similar to that of Edgar Morin. The complex is directly proportional to the organic principle of action: non-linear processes that obey the logic of living things. Science follows these propositions, and scientific revolutions have as a common factor the opening of black boxes to manufacture scientific facts, from which controversies emerge in an organic action dynamic. This narrative can be called the Ecology of Action within Science.

Ecology operates as a metaphorical loan from the Biological Sciences. These consigned relationships between the Fields of Knowledge help the narratives of phenomena that man traditionally has difficulty describing. Using the expression "ecology" is to understand that the role played by humans is relevant yet does not always occupy the centrality of scientific fact. Latour emphasizes this characteristic when dedicated to understanding how funding agencies participate in the paradigmatic revolutions he analyzes. Humans, laws, forms, and financing funds, among other actors, operate in them.

Understanding whom or what are the actants involved in a scientific fact are of questionable relevance, and the author states that attention can be directed to the strength or weakness of the ties established between these entities since the only common issue is to learn which associations are more robust and which are weaker—it is not about facing science, technology and society, but rather a range of more robust and more fragile associations that are dynamic and organic in any scientific field.

This dynamics of aggregation and disaggregation around the scientific fact will give rise to the movement of "translation," which, according to Latour, is the displacement between domains of knowledge or, as the author himself puts it, between science and technology and society. In addition to its linguistic meaning of translation (transposition from one language to another), it also has a geometric meaning (transposition from one place to another). Translating interests means, at the same time, offering new interpretations of those interests and channeling people in different directions.

Translation behaves as an action of displacement and appears to underpin the notion of transdisciplinarity. Based on Latour's interpretation of the circumference of action of scientific fact, it is interesting to see how facts, opinions, objects of study, researchers, and theories navigate the dynamic trails attributed between science disciplines. According to the author, realizing that the environment in which science takes place is organic (in the sense of following the logic of living things) generates the accumulation of knowledge. Scientists are spokespersons for their subjects of study. Therefore, Latour questions the tight separation between the research subject and the researched object, claiming that this expectation is not fulfilled unless the scientist does not get involved in the experiment, which could result in poor quality research. Latour advises the researchers to ask whom they speak for when a scientific cycle begins since they represent a knowledge area and field.

Introduction

This work derives from a doctoral thesis (Bonami, 2021) investigating the interface between educational success, human development, and digital technologies. Starting from concepts such as complexity, actor-network theory, action ecology, and hybridity, the central hypothesis here is that an excessive technicist conception of the mentioned interface can disfavor the debate on educational technologies and local tech development, treating them only as a tool or a means to reach an end. Considering that digital technologies expand human skills' horizons, this book proposes ten theoretical categories under which digital technologies are applied in education. These ten categories derive three abstraction clusters (instrument, power, and actants network), composing an evaluative framework to understand educational technologies and their possible applications: the SETA model.

The book begins with a prologue that sponsors the discussion around science development and paradigm shifts. Thus, the first chapter brings a State of the Art discussion around the main concepts that base this work, alongside an in-depth explanation of such theories and how they influence the thought around human development.

This foundation will guide the formulation of categories in the following chapters and discussions about a possible modular structure to illustrate the interface between the field of human development, education, and digital technology. In the second chapter, the ten categories will be presented and detailed, as well as the abstraction clusters (instrument, power, actants network) and how they shape the understanding of digital education. Furthermore, the third chapter discusses the possibility of conceptual models for knowledge, which embeds the presentation of the SETA model, featuring its application details in Amazonia/Brazil. Finally, it presents conclusions in the form of "final uncertainties," shedding light on the questions raised during the writing process.

Chapter 1

State of the Art

Thoughts on "Education" commonly focus on issues that permeate equitable access to quality learning. Since the 1990s, questions about education have covered aspects of digital technology and thinking about devices, majorly in their technical part, which can express an insufficiency regarding the potential for citizen empowerment these technologies can offer. Digital technology has the potential to build interactive structures so that the individual can observe oneself diluted in a communicational ecosystem. From an educational point of view, it means abandoning the technicist distinctions of digitization, subverting instrumental skills into amplified thinking about the power of the global web.

Today, teaching and learning are not just considering the interface between educators and students: it understands that the words designated in this process carry definitions that can hide the meanings of technology's power of human extension and the collective construction of knowledge. In the same way as the prefix, "post" is used to revoke categories of humanism [for example, in the expression post-humanism], the expression "literacy" lacks a post-look at its meaning. Its tense leads to the denotation of instrumental processes of apprehension of the world, leaving the individual's connective extension as a subjective factor and not the primary objective.

Presumably, digital technology leaves its instrumental dimension towards a perspective in which humans can [or not] control it. It establishes itself as a possibility to unveil other humanities in a self-eco-organized ecosystem. The credible repeal of anthropocentrism opens up a new type of connective intelligence by creating a space of ecological awareness.

This intelligence emanates from subjects that inhabit information simultaneously that they occupy physical space. Embarking on contemporary technology not only connects humans but a system of existing and traceable entities (through the emission of data). With the digital, it is possible to listen to the polyphony of actants in a network that speaks the complex melody of the biosphere composed by humans and non-humans [as explored in the prologue].

The convergence culture embraces the logic of appropriation between analogical and virtual spaces. Jenkins (2006) defines the convergence culture as where old and new media collide, corporate media integrates with the alternative, and production and consumption power meet. It does not depend directly on devices, as it is a logical process on the part of individuals in their collective and private interactions. At the base of the convergence culture, collective intelligence, as described by Lévy (1997), assumes a type of shared experience that arises from the collaboration of individuals in their diversities.

According to Lévy, it is an intelligence that is distributed everywhere, in which knowledge is in the interactions since no one knows everything, but everyone knows something. The ability of a community of thought is no longer shared but fundamentally collective knowledge, remaining available in this cloud of networked relationships. According to Lévy (1997), cyberspace results from a social movement with three guiding principles: interconnection, virtual communities, and collective intelligence.

A distinction is therefore drawn between shared knowledge and collective intelligence. The knowledge of a community of thought is no longer shared but fundamentally collective, remaining available in this cloud of networked relationships. The convergence culture, cyberculture, and collective intelligence can be seen as emergent properties between actants and forms of information processing. Along with the convergence of the various media, there is an apparent shift in cultural perception, making the convergence process complex and in constant metamorphosis due to its intrinsic association with a digital culture that influences the configuration of technological content.

When discussing knowledge shared in a network, one comes up against the concept of "social." The idea of society created by the West seems to limit the understanding of living in contemporaneity. Latour (1993) talks about the categorization of knowledge, a movement toward simplifying reasoning, splitting the human pole from the natural pole [as explored in the prologue]—which is altogether a western narrative of epistemology. With the chronological advance of modernity and post-modernity, this anthropocentric interpretation bias was put in check, bringing together the action of other non-human actants.

In this context, the very practice and thought about communication sciences changes, as it traditionally started from the principle and the transmission mechanisms of messages from human to human. With the advance of time and complexity, it began to add other network focuses beyond the humanist perspective. This discussion focuses on a critique of Cartesian thought of communicative direction and human action. Media ecology is no longer sufficient to describe the complexity of communicative action, suggesting that a communication ecology that is neither human-centric nor media-centric should be approached.

The anthropocentric concept built the imaginary of inhabiting in Western culture, characterized by the supposed separation between subject and environment. This idea was also questioned by some discoveries made in the first half of the last century, which highlighted the impossibility of separating the observing subject from the surrounding environment.

This so-called complexity presents itself as an ecology, being complexity here as Morin (2008) describes it, in a word that expresses the inability to define the antagonist of simplicity and is opposed to the principle of totality. Complex thinking can be multidimensional, based on a fabric of heterogeneous associations that constitute the phenomenal world. It deals with the reintegration (or reaggregation as stated by Latour) between anthropocentric and ecosystemic consciousness, assuming the dichotomy between balance and imbalance as a source of energy to direct action, which, according to Edgar Morin, is the logic of living things. It is an environment formulated as a self-eco-organized system, which denotes the organicity and complexity of actants.

According to Morin, a "system" is a unit composed of several integrated parts linked to the boundary and delimitation, forming the whole (greater than the sum of its parts). The author refers to a complex method for no longer systemic thinking, claiming systematic reasoning to be a fragmented and unidirectional knowledge. Going through its three principles (dialogical, recursion, and hologrammatical), it is possible to think of a network as a new ecology that proposes another type of complexity that is no longer systemic. The network gives the matter an informative architecture as an info structure, not abandoning its material dimension.

Morin is not content to criticize a systemic morphology of thought and therefore proposes "complex thinking" instead. This concept is built through its five volumes of "The Method," dealing with the exercise of an associative logic of contextual observation. By removing the term "complexity" from its denotative planning with the words "completeness" and "complexification," he positions "complexity" as a principle that manages "order and disorder" as the movement of a living organism itself.

Morin explains that at first glance, complexity is a fabric (complexus: what is woven together) of inseparably linked heterogeneous constituents: it poses the paradox of the one and the multiple. In a second moment, complexity is the fabric of events, actions, interactions, retroactions, determinations, and chance, which constitute the phenomenal world. But then, complexity presents itself with the disquieting features of the tangled, the inextricable, the disorder, the ambiguity, the uncertainty. Therefore, knowledge needs to order the phenomena, reject the disorder, remove the uncertain, select the elements of order and certainty, clarify, specify, distinguish, and hierarchize.

Complex thinking (a kind of associative logic that carries in its womb an impulse to manage imbalance) can be interpreted as a fertile basis for thinking about the "subject" in the social sphere and about carrying out the "action" in networks of interactions, a subject discussed within the scope of the production of the theorist Bruno Latour. Morin then introduces the concept of self-eco-organization to characterize the dynamics of interactions. The self-eco-organizing system has its individuality linked to relationships with the environment, therefore dependent. More autonomous, it is less isolated—it needs food, matter/energy, information, and order—bringing the environment inside as a co-organizing role.

Therefore, the self-eco-organizing system cannot be self-sufficient; it can only be logical when encompassing the external environment within itself. It cannot complete itself, close itself off, or be self-sufficient. The idea of complexity was much more present in current vocabulary than in scientific language, against clarification, simplification, and excessive reductionism. In science, however, complexity emerged without even saying its name in the nineteenth century; in microphysics and macrophysics, a complex relationship between the observer and the observed. Morin's argument around self-eco-organization supports his conception of transdisciplinarity, advocating the dissolution of scientific categories of knowledge.

There is uncertainty in the concept of science, a gap, an opening, and any claim to securely define the boundaries of science; any claim to the monopoly of science is therefore unscientific. The discussion on the categorization of knowledge plays a specific role in Bruno Latour's conception in his studies on the Actor-Network Theory, which will be addressed in the next section.

Actor-Network Theory

Bruno Latour launched in the 1980s (in association with other researchers such as Michel Callon and John Law) the Actor-Network Theory (ANT). Contrary to what the name (Actor-Network) might suggest, it is not a theory about contemporary connectivity or action in networks by actors connected by machinery interfaces. It is a study that starts from the argument that people (including scholars, theorists, and teachers) refer to the social as if it were a simple gender adjective such as "wooden," "steel," or "linguistic."

The acronym refers to the English word "ant," fitting perfectly with a blind, hard, and sniffer worker, the ant. Commonly, the "social" is defined through the radical itself. Sociology means (from the Greek/Latin) "science of the social," but there is an oxymoronic relationship between the "social" and the "science." The semantic construction of both concepts ran in opposite directions that led to a difficult meeting at a certain point in history, no matter how immersed they were in the human ecosystem. Latour (2007) proposes that, perhaps, these fields could come together again with the new technological advances and their penetration into everyday life. And in that, his prediction was assertive.

In an anecdotal tone, Latour (2005) points out that for "scientists," sociology is less critical, while for "sociologists," science is of lesser preponderance. His point is to show scientific facts in every "social event," just as one notices social influences in every "scientific event." There is a symbiosis between these epistemological fields, and barriers should therefore be broken so that they offer an integrated and transdisciplinary study between both areas. Yet, the attempt to define the "social" and "science" as inert fields has been, as the author himself says, "a comedy of errors." His criticism of watertight epistemological areas directly concerns what the author calls hybrid or almost-human bodies or almost-objects between the social and natural poles.

With the ANT, the Social Sciences have a new set of objects to be studied. Latour proposed including non-human actions in science, placing actants as protagonists of discourses in the social domain. Some authors disapprove of

Latour's hypothesis, deeming it unlikely that scientists, especially from natural sciences, would abandon their distinctions between humans and non-humans.

As his research progresses, Latour finds the nature of entities (human or non-human) increasingly irrelevant. Furthermore, hybridity assumes its power when it considers the action's ignition point to be the essential phenomenon and not the nature of the agent. It is an attention to the course of action and its connection to the efforts of other actants. The notion of actant in the ANT encompasses any type of entity that appears on the network to mediate an action. This concept becomes relevant in the Information Age, in which interfaces and computers are increasingly autonomous in their functions.

The word "Network" is an informal way of associating these agents, acting as a flow of translations that can be tracked, aggregated, and active (what does not act, does not exist in it; if it does, there are traces, recurrences, confluences, aggregations). It is not made of threads or fibers but the trace left by a moving actor. The ANT is, in general terms, an equalization between humans and non-humans, without clinging to the essences of these two types of entities but considering their aggregations.

Latour's reasoning is about science not being the study of an object but rather a study of the action of scientists, as it is situated in practice and not in theory. As actants can be considered trapped puppets, their condition is not the element that the researcher needs to cling to. Their actions directly depend on the researcher's ability to let them act. For that, it is necessary to emancipate them (or loosen their strings), putting the scientist in a position of a puppeteer. In other words, it is by multiplying connections with the outside that science can perceive how facts are being built.

In 2012, Latour launched as a post-ANT the "Enquête sur les Modes d'Existence" (Survey on the Modes of Existence), a survey of researchers from parts of the world using information and communication technologies. In this work from 2012, Latour claims that it is necessary to understand which beings are appropriate for different areas of knowledge, while in his reference from 2007, he talks about the importance of the course of action and its development, making the actant a mere mediating entity or intermediary of this path. He also assumes that, contrary to what was proposed in 2007, ANT is not a methodology but one of the ways of existence, of knowing the truth about the world.

Latour calls modes of existence the thread of existence aware of the various regimes of truth, based on the title of Souriau's (2009) book, "Modes d'Existence." Modes are forms of particular existence, how something relates to the world or the conditions of the interaction of an entity. In Latour's words, Souriau argues that there are not multiple ways to talk about a world but various ways to approach worlds (attention to the plural). These modes of existence allow the moderns to be offered a more realistic description than Western reasoning. Latour hypothesizes that each mode of existence makes it possible to respect specific ontologies.

Each mode requires the encounter of distinct beings, which must be approached in their languages. The classic question "what is the essence of technology, science, religion, and so on?" becomes "which beings are appropriate for technology, science, religion, and how have Moderns tried to approach them?" What Latour seeks to know is "how can the reproduction of these modes be justified when civilization claims that it was conceived based on two categories, object, and subject?" His idea of hybridity may be correct, but it was conceived in a social spectrum built on the distinction of these entities. Latour explicitly discusses the failure of the network as an instrument.

According to the author, the network leaves something to be desired, as it breaks down the associations but does not consider the variety of connections. Therefore, it is no longer the only way to describe the associations (for this reason, there are other ways of understanding the world beyond the ANT). The ANT does not treat the network as a digital artifact, outlining the Social as a set of aggregations observed by the researcher and proposes that the ontological separation between the observing subject and the observed object is increasingly less relevant in scientific research.

The context of complexity leads the actor to act; it creates an ecology of tracks and textures woven by moving actant fibers. For Latour, using the word actor is never sure about who acts or what in ecology, making it possible to act. He considers that, in place of the word "social," one can use "collectives" of actants and entities that constantly aggregate and disaggregate according to the dimensions of the controversy of their members.

However, there are other ways of aggregation, such as affectivity or consensus (and not just controversy, as he would defend); thus, whether digital and aggregative networks (as Latour conceives them) can be considered equivalent because it is about thinking and expressing the non-social qualities that happen in the context of connective ecologies and trying to describe the interactions in a digital, reticular, and ecological way.

In his Paris Invisible City project, he suggests that digitization innovates to allow visualizations that were not previously available since networks have physical and informational (virtual) dimensions. However, Latour does not elaborate on the digitization debate, and he admits this himself. Nevertheless, in the 21st century, it seems possible to assume that aggregations of collectives can think about the digital more than its visualization, yet as a way of acting qualitatively different from what was seen before and offline.

The benefit of bringing some of Latour's work and reasoning is expanding the set of actants scientific hypotheses can observe and developing a deeper understanding of how researchers dance between knowledge fields. Thus, the creation of transdisciplinary areas such as Science Technology and Society (STS) welcomes studies like this to have a shelter and to be able to exist without being in constant displacement (2014). Furthermore, when the SETA model (to be presented next) was first created, much of its employment fell into the Social-Technical realm of action, which can dissolve the distinctions between macro-social level and laboratory science experiment, breaking the insulation barriers allowing scientists and scientific facts to breath.

Hybridism, Ecology, and the Question of Technique

The term "hybridism" characterizes contemporary societies, especially Latin American ones. After the world wide web, the use of the term is expanded to refer to the convergence of media in the digital world: it is the mixture of languages in hypermedia (the junction of hypertext and multimedia that defines the language of networks). Recently, hybridization has broadened to refer to the interconnection of physical circulation spaces with the virtual information spaces to which users connect.

According to Santaella (2008), hybrid, hybridism, and hybridization are radicals that characterize contemporary society's facets; they concern social formations, cultural mixtures, media convergence, and an eclectic combination of languages and signs. In a metaphorical import from Biological Sciences (since hybridization refers to the production of genetically modified plants and animals). The hybrid denotes senses of miscegenation, whether of species, technologies, or words, being the hybrid nature in the constitution of spaces as "interstitial": whose borders between physical and digital spaces which compose connectivity are diluted into traditional distinctions and patterns.

Interstitial spaces refer to the borders between physical and digital spaces, composing connected enviroments. The traditional distinction between physical spaces, on the one hand, and digital spaces, on the other, is broken. Thus, an interstitial or hybrid space occurs when it is no longer necessary to "leave" the physical space to connect with digital environments. As a result, these edges become fuzzy and no longer completely distinguishable.

Hybrid spaces combine the physical and the digital in a social environment created by the mobility of users connected via mobile communication devices. The nuances between hybridity and the dissolution of physical and virtual barriers seem to structure the postmodern mind in a hybrid architecture of aggregations. Thus, digital technology can be interpreted as a set of interaction architectures: the focus is not on technological functionality but on the types of aggregations it can structure between human and non-human actants.

The word "hybrid" carries dissonant meanings in its bosom (which Santaella said about the benefits of using a "borrowed" term from the Biological Sciences) and the advantage of using a time loaded with equivocality. However, what seems to be engaging in the study of hybridity is not the hybrid object (as a result) but the trajectory of these discrete practices in diluting their identity borders and becoming interstitial entities: in other words, the interest in the study of hybridization is this process that appears to dilute the human-centric domain over technique and other beings.

Felice (2021) relies on the dissolution of Western ontological patterns that distinguish technique from knowledge (as proposed by Aristotle in the complementarity between episteme and teknee) and bases his argument on Heidegger (1977) about a human who is not prepared for a world dominated by technique, placing science as a form of production beyond man. Heidegger proposes that the essence of the technique is not in technique but in man since it is not an instrument but an unveiling process (of discovering the truth).

At the same time, man does not control the technique, however much he claims to do (Heidegger exemplifies this with the Atomic Bomb event in

World War II). The method doesn't come from science; science stems from technique, and together they intensify each other. Man, with its wisdom for a long time, created technologies to improve the survival condition of the species. These inventions do not always originate in science; they mostly come from man's intervention (of conscious action) to supply a demand.

In confluence with McLuhan's (1969) studies, thinking about technique (and, by extension, technology) as an extension of the central nervous system and perception being metaphorically associated with an in-depth massage of the senses. A new dimension of technique emerges, which is no longer only material but also immaterial, which affects the ways of perceiving the world. Cybernetics elaborates on extra-human communication through computers, being itself the extension of language to machines.

Technology leaves its instrumental dimension towards a perspective in which humans cannot control it. It establishes itself as a possibility to unveil other humanities in a self-eco-organized ecosystem (as mentioned before). It is presumably the repeal of anthropocentric humanism, which opens up a new type of connective intelligence by creating a space of ecological awareness.

From this perspective, communication ecology began to be applied to explain the interconnectedness of materiality and immateriality in communicative environments. As a term from the biological sciences, ecology is used to understand how living and non-living entities interact with their immediate environments. Transposed to the human and social sciences, an ecological framework seeks to understand the same behaviors between human beings, technical systems, linguistic processes, and a host of other objects and entities.

In the 1970s, for example, the Norwegian philosopher Arne Næss pioneered the Deep Ecology Movement—DEM (Næss, 2016). Based on the work of Baruch Spinoza, the DEM begins with an assumption that all living entities, regardless of whether they have instrumental use for human ends or not, have inherent value. This environmental, philosophical composition responds to the tendency to reduce nature to an object excluded from the anthropological domain.

This dissatisfaction is directed at modern sciences, which constantly look for abstract and universal structures in nature without fully understanding the lived experiences of being-in-the-world. The views embodied in the ecological perspective focus on the need to develop a broader understanding of the interrelationships of animate and inanimate entities. The approach placed ecological issues in the philosophical discussion with the view that human beings cannot be separated from a broader understanding of ecology. Ethical predispositions for ecological development can also be applied to human behavior.

However, DEM is not without its limitations. Bonami; Nemorin (2020), for example, argue that the approach can tend to be too "cosmological." In this view, ecology should focus its attention on "interaction," not just any type of interaction or stakeholder. It is not a random science in which anything can be analyzed. Instead, the concept can be used as a complete procedure for tracking interactions to understand entities' actions deeply. In a related way, DEM speaks of a radical ecological worldview.

Bonami; Nemorin (2020) argues that the movement is not just non-anthropocentric but anti-anthropocentric, which poses a problem since human beings are an animal species like any other. The author introduces critics of the DEM through ecofeminism (feminist ecology), discussing the patriarchal conceptual framework characterized by hierarchical value thinking, giving more excellent status to what is traditionally identified as masculine than what is usually identified as feminine. This structure generates a logic of domination that serves to legitimize inequality.

Furthermore, ecology is not a struggle against human interaction but oppressive interactions. DEM wants to unmask the ideology behind anthropocentrism. Ecofeminism analyzes the distribution of power dominance. While ecofeminism understands the problem from an anthropocentric perspective, it adds a crucial dimension to the logic and domination of history against particular beings and systems.

Despite its limitations, the DEM has made significant contributions to disseminating its defining image of human actions, describing the ecological crisis resulting from the anthropocentric humanism central to contemporary ideologies. In other words, environmental challenges stem from the arrogance of the human imagination, like nature's central nervous system or brain. An ecological approach can be used to highlight and challenge issues of power imbalance.

In this work, ecology, as a concept borrowed from the biological sciences, fulfills the role of expressing and describing the relationships and interactions between actants in the fields of knowledge between digital technology and communication and education. As seen in the paragraphs before, actants are entities (human and non-human) related to forming fields of knowledge. Therefore, their tracking and study become a relevant topic in this book. The connection of the concept with the study of technology takes place in two areas: one (as already explored) in the potential to describe the interactions between actants; and another in the description of the senses of dominance that alternate between the figure of a human and the existence of technique. This second aspect will be the basis for further understanding of the categories and clusters explored.

Chapter 2

Digital Education and Abstraction Clusters

In the early 20th century, studies on the impact of connectivity sought to understand sociotechnical systems' nature, form, and implications. In short, the objective was to understand the materialities incorporated in the process and the different roles. Using the structure of the materiality of communication, scholars have argued that humans emerged from a physical world to inhabit a symbolic atmosphere, where material content is understood (Habermas, 1991). The subject's presence in a dubious sphere, both online and offline, made aspects of the fields of communication, education, and technology intersect at a semantic level.

Dialogue at a semantic level touches on the history of electronic systems, the launch of the Internet, and how this qualitatively alters informational cycles. Luciano Floridi (2014) talks about the disruptive qualities of technological transformations, arguing that the "news" is an invitation to rethink the present and the future in a technologized way. In other words, Floridi (2014) suggests a redesign of the conceptual vocabulary and how the world is meant and understood. Nevertheless, the author defines the separation of three ages of development of human knowledge: Prehistory, History, and Hyper-History.

In his work, he defines Prehistory as the processes of knowledge from the Bronze Age (expressed by the development of writing in Mesopotamia and other regions of the world) to the Information Age (when, according to him, is the period of the story). He suggests that both History and Hyperhistory appear as adverbs: they say how people live, not when or where. Hyper-History's dependence on Information and Communication Technologies (ICT) is created the Information Cycle (Figure 1). Information is the nucleus (in direct reference to cells and molecules) orbited by procedures and steps, developing the idea of information as a living organism that is not autonomous but can be recycled and managed.

The idea of information as a living process embraces the concept of Complexity. As mentioned in the last chapter, Complex thinking can be described as multi-dimensional or as the aggregation between anthropocentric and ecosystemic thinking. The imbalance between both schools of thought (anthropocentric and ecological) highlights an unbalanced dynamic, an imbalance that provides energy for the information cycle. Information follows an organic dynamic, and it is prudent to view it as an autonomous entity with functions similar to living beings (a process associated with Aristotle's conception of "autopoiesis", as explored by Maturana; Varela, 1987).

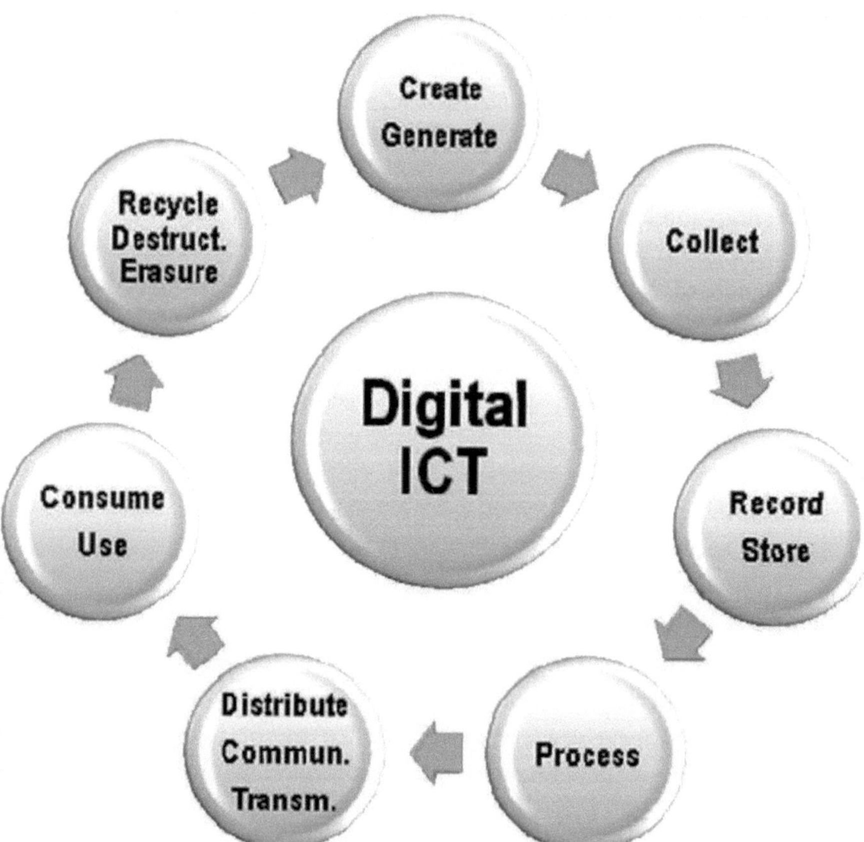

Figure 1: the life cycle of information. Source: Floridi, 2014.

As explained in Chapter 01, as Morin clarifies the concept of Complexity, a systemic environment is not the entities alone but their connections and possible integrations, an idea close to the studies of the interaction between humans and computers. In Human-Computer Interaction (HCI), Information and Communication Technologies (ICT) create and facilitate communication between users and computer systems. To mention ICT is possibly to reconsider that computers don't compute and phones don't make calls. Humans perform these actions, or at least until the autonomous algorithms begin. These systems deal with data, whereas humans intertwine in a network of systems and rely on their ability to assess (based on Big Data).

In other words, to understand technology, the first step is to consider that networks are not stable and linear but rather complex and dynamic. The field of communication intersects areas of knowledge such as philosophy, sociology, computer science, education, and ecology.

Recurrent discussions in the field of communication argue that the digitization of the 21st century provides a qualitative change in reality, whose dimensions and meanings seem not to be fully understood and expressed through the philosophical categories and language produced by Western culture. Historically, the human inherits the world view through the Aristotelian separation of the episteme between human, nature, and technique. The idea of society, inspired by the development of social sciences in the modern era, is based on the Aristotelian ontology that reports the social as formed by the sets of "socius" and the individual as a political animal, capable of administering and controlling its world.

Similarly, given the spread of forms of automated intelligence, platform, and blockchain interactions, the narrative based on the centrality of the human and its autopoiesis, allowed the reckoning of technologies and the environment in a co-dependent way. The advent of new information architecture—no longer based on media, broadcasters, content, and channels but organized in networks and interactive ecologies that enable the collaborative construction of content and information—is now inhabited by humans and non-humans (see section "Actor-Network Theory").

The digitization process is no longer a communicative or media sphere phenomenon but has become a holistic ecosystem. More than a virtualization procedure, transforming things and relationships into data unleashed a computerized dimension of reality based on algorithmic processing, data, and information flow. The introduction of the set of non-human entities as members and living actors of the society constitutes the pretext and the opportunity to re-question their morphology and, above all, to rethink the western idea of society (Societas).

Prigogine and Stengers (1997) argue that reducing social architecture to individuals influenced the conception of relationships and affected the relationship between humans and the environment, determining the latter's consideration as something external to the social. Both Prigogine, Stengers (1997), and Latour (2005) propose that even throughout the history of the development of social sciences, the meaning and architecture of society maintained their anthropomorphic and anthropocentric structure.

Similarly, Serres (1995) rejects the Western idea of the anthropomorphic character of the social, based on the distinction between man and the environment. In his book "The Natural Contract" (1995), the philosopher defends overcoming the Enlightenment conception of the social, based on anthropomorphic knowledge and the centrality of human action. The criticism developed by the French philosopher was not only focused on the beginning of society but the idea of ecology external to man. The word "environment" here assumes that humans are not at the center of a system of actants around them since the thought of human centrality has a problematic genealogy, which became clearer since Giordano Bruno's trial in the 15th Century.

Following Serres' (1994) critique, Felice (2017) argues that in the context of transgenic digital networks, it is prudent to rethink digital and social inclusion contexts—redefining what is thought of as "internal" or "external" to networks of interactions. In addition to questioning the Western idea of society, it is essential to rethink the exact composition of the common. The latest generations of connections network not only people and technologies (digital social networks) but objects (IoT), territories (Geographic Information Systems—GIS), and biodiversity (Internet of Everything), transforming aspects of reality into data and bits.

The Internet has taken on meta dimensions, digitizing part of the biosphere, creating an incalculable amount of data, and connecting the different sizes of metaverses. Various levels of connection and other forms of sensors extend beyond the borders of technology, which is no longer limited to a network of information transmitted by computers. Internet is no longer a technical network and is no longer just a network of people and citizens: it is the advent of a new planetary connection, but different from the one that united the knowledge of human intelligence to the world. The new forms of connection established after the metaverse and digitizing the biosphere transform citizens and inhabitants of cities, countries, and nations into inhabitants of bit galaxies.

An ecological dimension of the global network, which introduces humans and non-humans into the same communicational bath (vis à vis Lévy,1997), has the potential to establish new parameters for understanding the interactions between humans and machinery processes. Some fields can benefit from this discussion, such as the area of communication and education, and this is where this books heads next.

Digital technologies' crossroads: platforms and Big Data

Contemporary science discusses the accumulation of factual data, which seems to drive technological innovations so that they can create credible processes, removing this responsibility from human curation. A systemic and decentralized structure brought the possibility of accelerating innovation cycles since more actants are involved in the process of creating values and, more specifically, the emergence of digital platforms that, since the year 2000, began to lead the reconfigurations not only from the economic scenario but also social, political and cultural (Parker et al., 2016).
Expanding the discussion, Van Dijk (2018) presents a broader and more complex understanding of which platforms are impacting and converging with institutions (whether public or private), forcing a readjustment of democratic and legal structures, which the author named as "Platform Society."

This expression refers to the omnipresent and percussive character of these architectures that do not represent a parallel structure that reflects society (that is, another virtual reality, which mimics "concrete" social structures) but which are, precisely, producing the new structures in which people live, putting into confrontation private and collective benefits, corporate gains and public interests. Hence the indication is not to study them in isolation, separated from the social and the political spheres, but in communion with interdependent layers of global infrastructure in development since the turn of the last century (Dijck, 2018).

According to Accoto (2020), the platforms' codes and algorithms do not function as tools facilitating online interaction but as performative technologies that project the future. In other words, the code is not used solely to record or store information but guides a double-action (from the code to the machine and from the device to the world). The code is not conceived in terms of what happened (as in literary, television, and film narratives) but produces what is about to happen.

Meanwhile, algorithms collect, analyze, group, and transmit information according to their logical and logistical system, linked to the platform operators' business model that seems to shape society's organization. Understanding the qualitative transformations promoted by platforms in education seems relevant to articulating a mechanism inherent to them: datafication.

Datafication is the mechanism that enables the platform in a network to transform aspects of the world into quantifiable data. In this sense, user interactions on digital platforms can be captured, algorithmically processed, and packaged in profiles, allowing the development of prediction models and behavior analysis in real-time. Datafication intensifies the commodification process, which is the platform's ability to turn objects, activities, emotions, and ideas into commodities (as the mass of data is collected and processed, it offers insights into users' interests, preferences, and needs). Finally, the connection between datafication and commodification drives selection (or curation) mechanisms, allowing the combination of users with personalized services.

The ethical dimension of these activities increases with the lack of transparency in data processing. Data has been shared between humans and systems for much of human history. For example, the first identity cards were created in Ancient Rome, and the Order of Westminster in England created the passport during the reign of Henry VIII. However, historical processes of accumulating personal and public data seemed to disregard the level of transparency with which this data was operated and why it was collected. Contemporary tensions around the data set issued every minute gain strength once citizens understand that most of their acts, choices, and preferences become informational products for something or someone.

Therefore, it seems interesting to understand these systems, how they operate, and the tensions surrounding their performance. The following paragraphs will explore what Big Data, Artificial Intelligence, and Blockchain are and how these technologies relate to education and the platformization phenomenon. Artificial Intelligence (AI) and Blockchain emerged in the Zettabyte era, which means that intelligent machine performance is required due to Big Data. The generations since 2014 are facing the Zetta flood, which describes the byte tsunami and AI becoming a natural development of an intelligent system that needs to deal with this wave. This is why both terms (AI and Big Data) are complementary.

Despite the phenomenon's importance, it is still unclear what Big Data means. The term was first introduced in 1989 by Erik Larson in an article published in the Washington Post on dealing with the amount of mail received daily (Larson, 1989). However, theorists attribute the Big Data concept to John R. Mashey in his article "Big Data and the Next Wave of InfraStress Problems, Solutions, Opportunities,"[1] recognizing the demand for analytical models to process data.

References contributed to the development of the term until, in 2012, the first set of legal regulations for public and sensitive data was released with General Data Protection Regulation 2012. In Brazil, the General Data Protection Law (Federal Government, "L13709", 2019) was launched in 2019 and followed similar guidelines to the European Commission. However, the problem here is not about the amount of data, which suggests that solutions should be updated: it does not refer to processing capacity (since this activity occurs on demand) but to epistemological issues of small patterns that analyze Big Data.

Small patterns represent the frontier of innovation and competition, from science to business, governance to social policy, and security to protection, which is why the patterns should be small to improve their processing speed (as the data is voluminous, small patterns clump them together to speed up their synthesis). Small patterns can be risky, as they can predict choices and events, which runs counter to ethical principles of information. Another

---

[1] More informations at: https://web.stanford.edu/class/ee380/9798win/lect08.html

characteristic of data is the volume (one zettabyte can store all the information in human history).

Figure 2: connecting dots image. Source: Getty Images, 2022.

The Big Data Taxonomy Report released in 2021 introduces three limits to the speed of data growth: thermodynamics, intelligence, and memory. This is why attempting to approach AI as one of the solutions for Big Data is worrisome, since intelligence is one of its limitations, as there is not enough storage for all the data (memory limitation). Søe (2018) warns that the main problem with this particular field is epistemological. The prospect that the amount of data is an issue is misleading since the first question is how late humans became aware of its existence. But why are small patterns such a big problem? Floridi (2014) answers this question with a dot-connection figure illustration: in a dot-to-dot exercise, the more data points you connect, the better the pattern. Unless one connects all the dots, it is impossible to know the final figure.

The thing about Big Data is that you need standards to try to analyze them (like finding a needle in a haystack). The integration between Big Data and Artificial Intelligence is that datasets must create their intelligence to identify where the needle is. However, not all data is essential. Floridi (2014) points out that perhaps half of them are insignificant, while the other half are valuable. The role of small patterns is to know which is the right half to analyze. Once the data is mapped, there is an aggregation feature (essential data that can lead systems to understand their customers/readers and even predict their choices). As a methodological procedure, small patterns are significant when they correlate with relevant assets, including the absence/silence of the analyzed data.

The ability to advance with AI algorithms can predict possible behaviors and results (such as the cookie system and its analysis of screen scrolling and clicks performed by the user). However, one of the main challenges for advancing AI, in addition to ethical issues, is the systematization and organization of valuable data. To contribute to this discussion, the following paragraphs explain what Artificial Intelligence is and in which contexts it can be applied.

Artificial Intelligence and Blockchain: a brief review

Artificial Intelligence (AI) has been a topic on the radar of theorists and experts since the 1950s, and, to this day, discussions sustain some difficulty in defining it. Studies began in 1956 when John McCarthy mentioned the term in a seminar at Dartmouth University in the United States[2]. Despite this record, it is possible to find investigations since 1951 associated with the area of Genetics in Biological Sciences. Also, in 1951, Alan Turing published the study "Computing Machinery and Intelligence" (Turing, 1950), in which he presented the "Imitation Game," also known as the "Turing Test": a set of questions in which it is possible to define whether the respondent is human or machine.

Recent literature reflects such distinctions and goes into the merits of how AI can be applied. The International Telecommunication Union (ITU) has released the "AI for Good Global Summit 2018" report that develops the concept of a system that does not replace human intelligence. Similarly, the

---

[2] Official documents about the seminar can be found at the link: https://250.dartmouth.edu/highlights/artificial-intelligence-ai-coined-dartmouth

Organization for Economic Co-operation and Development (OECD) positions AI as a structure that increases human intelligence potential.

Floridi (2014) discusses the applications of AI, arguing that successful systems are those with an environment molded around them. In other words, systems that respond to specific purposes (Floridi gives an example of robots that mow grass—how good they are at this task—but they wouldn't take on the role of a refrigerator well). This is known as a frame problem. According to Floridi, AI does not take a descriptive or prescriptive approach to the world: it investigates the logical and mathematical coercion that makes it possible to build artifacts and interact with them effectively.

AI is related to Blockchain, as it allows the construction of artifacts that make authentication processes automatic. Blockchain is a technology that generates a report containing transaction and action history, called blocks that are connected through end-to-end encryption (data and user security and protection system). These blocks with transaction histories generate seals secured by cryptography and updated in real-time. The foundation of its design is the resistance to modification of the data in these seals. It is commonly defined as an open, distributed ledger that stores transactions between interacting parties to be permanently verified. The Blockchain is operated by a network of peers that adhere to inter-node communication protocols that validate new blocks as they are added to the original products to apply the distributed ledger design.

Blockchain technology's origin is nebulous since it is unclear whether its creator Satoshi Nakamoto is a person or a group of actants (since his identity is unknown). The invention of bitcoin (or cryptocurrency) became the first case of a digital currency that does not require validation by any country's Central Banks. Blockchain's distributed ledger encryption technology makes this subversion of the economic order.

Bitcoin's design inspired other applications, and Blockchain became an application for payment tracking. The first work using block cryptography and distributed ledger date from 1991 by Stuart Haber and W. Scott Stornetta to implement a system of seals that could not be tampered with (Haber & Stornetta, 1991). However, the first cryptocurrency application was made by Nakamoto in 2008. Blockchain technology enables the Internet of Values (IoV), a secure platform, registry, or database where transaction values are stored and exchanged without traditional mediators.

In the case of an application outside the financial sphere, such as journalism or education, Blockchain allows decentralized transactions on the web, making it possible to maintain a search and upload record. This optimizes the management of personal information, using this data in an encrypted form in a way that preserves sensitive data. The scenario seems to be thriving for launching educational and journalistic institutes with enough operational capabilities to manage vast databases.

Despite its potentiality, Blockchain carries risks along with its promise of cryptography. Perhaps because of insecurity coupled with the complexity of its system, technology (at least in the humanities field) is a factor that makes it difficult to develop metrics for its evaluation and validation. Possible integration between education and communication sciences would be through real-time stamps. For example, the "open badge" is a technical infrastructure with specifications recognizing achievements with a digital icon (such as a medal). The Mozilla Foundation created the open badge in 2012 (coming in version 2.0 in 2018)[3].

The specification is a method of packet information about user achievements stored in a cloud that can be shared between platforms, ensuring that sensitive data is adequately protected. This would contribute to the user experience as the user would be able to take control of their data themselves. The platform could use this information transparently without denouncing its market strategy. The idea of a distributed registry is to create a space where relevant information is secured, generating medals that can add value. This value can be symbolic (as in knowledge construction) or material (in collaboration or even financial). This application is an example of online course platforms such as Coursera, Udacity, and EdX[4].

Therefore, the context of the use of Blockchain is situated in two areas: the first in understanding how the technology works even without applying it, and the second in the area of skills and user management. In this case, the Blockchain would operate as a cloud that, in addition to storing data in transparency and quantity, could offer counterparts to the user experience: a gamification process and the provision of medals. Gamification applies game

---

[3] More information at the link: https://support.mozilla.org/pt-BR/kb/o-que-e-o-projeto-open-badges-da-mozilla 8 More information at the link: https://pt.coursera .org/
[4] More information at the link: https://www.udacity.com/
More information at the link: https://www.edx.org/

logic in operations that are not configured as games: fulfillment of stages, trophies, and awards.

At the same time, it would be possible to organize this data into blocks, which could be checked and authenticated in real-time by any part of this interaction. In the case of communication and education, this could be implemented both in the training part (media and information literacies) and in the certification part (automatic authentication seals for certificates according to the paths users walk on platforms).

Despite its popularity in the financial sphere, Blockchain has significant value in recognizing the acquisition and development of knowledge. When this factor is combined with the protection of sensitive data, it has the potential to address solutions to educational, media, social, and even political issues. The European Commission conducted in early 2018 the Action Plan for Digital Education, which had as its protagonist the awareness and application of Blockchain technology, which would be used in issuing, checking, and validating certificates at all educational levels. One of the action plan topics includes automatic information checking, optimizing machine learning algorithms, and AI when creating real-time stamps with certification. However, a clause was added to the rejection of censorship in this process, demanding a guarantee that media and informational content were evaluated by Blockchain logic (distributed record of blocks in the chain) and not by content screening.

When reviewing the technologies above, from the phenomenon of platformization to Big Data, AI, and Blockchain, the question of how this intersects in the theoretical sphere with the field of education emerges. Some approaches could go to the dimension of its application through the enumeration of techniques and devices that could be used for a supposed improvement of teaching and its respective systems. However, this work understands that the issue at the intersection of these fields of knowledge occurs in the semantic sphere, which suggests an investigation into what digital technology means when studied in education, especially in the Global South.

Ten categories to understand digital education

In 2020, this research was faced with the following question: how is it possible to explain the interface between digital technology and education in the

Global South? The first step was systematically reviewing research papers and journal articles to understand how this relationship occurs.

This research considers that digital technology in interface with education can be explained and studied in ten categories to understand the complexities embedded in these systems. These categories were extracted from the Social Sciences, Communication Sciences, Education, and Digital Technology systematic review between 2016 and 2020. To reach such a conclusion, search, selection, sorting, reading, and synthesis procedures were explored in four scientific portals[5], resulting in the deep investigation of 80 research articles (out of 5,100 selected for superficial review). The ten categories were grouped into three sets that express levels of abstraction to understand digital technology in the educational field.

The systematic review of the selected materials made it possible to codify different theoretical levels of discussion via topic modeling, thus producing the categories above. With the encoding of pertinent information from each document, the PRISMA (Preferred Reporting Items for Systematic Reviews and Meta-Analyses)[6] model was employed, consisting of items based on evidence from a vast collection of data from relevant literature.

With PRISMA and topic modeling, each article was positioned in tables to extract the following data:

- Information on indexing (authorship and its origin, year and publication vehicle, title, abstract, and keyword);
- What the article is about;
- How does it relate to the interface between education and digital technology; and

---

[5] CAPES (administered by the Ministry of Science and Technology of Brazil); Educational Resources Information Center (ERIC), sponsored by the Department of Education in the United States; Scopus multidisciplinary database, a member of Elsevier; UCL Library Online Portal.
http://www-periodicos-capes-gov-br.ezl.periodicos.capes.gov.br/index.php
More information at: https://eric.ed.gov/
More information at: https://www.scopus.com/
More information at: https://www.ucl.ac.uk/library/
[6] The PRISMA model is predominantly used in the health sciences, but it can be applied in this research as a method of evaluating data collected through theoretical literature review and interviews.

- Words and concepts are used to define this interface (quantitative analysis).

Among the ten categories in which the articles fit the study of digital technology and education, some considerations are essential:

- All categories' titles are listed in the following table;
- Categories were extracted according to topics modeling; and
- Each article read in-depth was fitted into one or more categories.

#	Ten categories to explain and understand digital education
1	Digital Technology as a Potential to Solve Education Problems
2	Digital Technology as a Logical Operation
3	Digital Technology as a Tool
4	Digital Technology as a New Paradigm of Post-Modern Societies
5	Digital Technology as a new Education Paradigm
6	Digital Technology as an Extension of Human Perception
7	Technique as an autonomous entity (Big Data, AI, Blockchain, IoT)
8	Digital Technology under an Ecological Approach
9	Digital Technology as a Distributed Narrative among Actants
10	Digital Technology as a Humanocentric Narrative

Table 1: Ten categories to explain and understand digital education

#	Explanation
1	It presents digital technology as an accelerator of empowerment for learners and educators, allowing the improvement of digital skills. The word "potentially" is followed by the word "possibility", suggesting that digital technology offers new opportunities to those who reach them.
2	It deals with digital technology as logical skills and knowledge groups, alongside language learning, enabling the individual to develop these logic abilities. Logic literacies are commonly associated with mathematics or physics learning—but here implies that principles—originally from mathematical education—are omnipresent in all disciplines in contact with digital technology.
3	It interprets digital technology as a tool, an instrument or as a means to an end. It deals, therefore, with technology as an object to be dominated by the human being to achieve personal, professional, socioeconomic, and cultural goals.
4	It offers the interpretation of digital technology as a new paradigm for post-modern society, promoting: • The dissolution of the industrial economic scenario, opening room for new abilities and new employment possibilities; • The platform society era; • Urban gentrification with new arrangements brought by platforms; and • Data culture and literacy in education.
5	It interprets digital technology as a new educational paradigm, promoting hybrid learning between • Formal and informal settings of education; • Classical teaching (instruction); • The analog dissemination of knowledge (such as books); • Personalized learning; • Project-based learning; and • Shared production of knowledge.

6	It presents digital technology as an extension of the human being [promoting a "deep massage" among the 5 senses] based on Marshall McLuhan's studies. That way, technology cannot be defined in its use as a means to an end, as the human being changes and develops when in contact with it.
7	It interprets technique and algorithms as autonomous entities capable of creating and reproducing knowledge and information, arguing against the philosophical conception of the human figure as the only entity capable of intelligence and creation. Here the principle of autopoiesis would be extended not only to living creatures but to any actant that performs in a network or system.
8	It considers technology more engaging than its aspects around the human context, taking into account the life story, the environment and the sustainability narrative, based on the ecology of action as a concept of entropy.
9	It describes the interactions between humans and non-humans under a flat ontology (based on Latour's Network-Actor Theory), in which the human is not the only one to master the technique. In fact, the nature of the agent is not important, but its actions and how they aggregate with other agents.
10	It describes interactions between humans and the technique underlying human relevance in digital manipulation. This authorizes the human being to create, change, transform and share technical phenomena. This perspective expands the technique as something required to achieve a goal in which resource manipulation comes from an industrial (or historical) perspective.

Table 2: Description of ten categories to explain and understand digital education

The grouped categories suggest sets of abstraction between the interface between education and digital technology. The groups can repeat more than one category among them, and the objective of their creation is to understand how digital technology is being studied in educational projects or initiatives. The three clusters suggest levels of understanding about the status quo of studying digital technologies in education. Reflections on technique and decentralization of human activity seem to contribute to a broader understanding of the relationship between education and digital technology.

Abstraction clusters

Potter (2017) reflects on the intersection between digital technologies and education with a metaphor from the novel "The City and the City" (Miéville, 2010), which tells the story of two cities that coexist in the same space, sharing streets and even buildings in "crossed areas." In the story, it is illegal for the citizens of these cities to recognize when they see themselves. They spend their lives policed by an organization that enforces the law of "compulsory invisibility." As children, the citizens of these fictional places walked along shared streets, but gradually they learned not to 'see' each other, so they made it natural when they grew up to live in a place with two intersecting areas. Potter (2017) describes this crime thriller by analogy with the intersection of fields of knowledge, arguing the existence of parallel epistemological fields that are rehearsed not to see orthogonal areas.

Potter's perception is that in recent years, theories and writers, disciplines, and parallel perspectives occupy the same spaces as in the work of Miéville (2010). Sometimes, such fields of knowledge develop and build empires of knowledge while avoiding recognizing this co-presence. These epistemological tensions, sometimes even naturalized in the scientific structure, intersect with the concept of "field" (Bourdieu, 1986), especially in describing social actors autonomously occupying discrete domains. This phenomenon is established in education and digital technologies, which seems to be the imposition of barriers that make related fields incommunicable.

Crossing the barriers between knowledge areas is called an exercise of abstraction, and the groupings created in this work suggest levels at which this crossing occurs. The interface becomes the bridge built through the process of abstraction, enabling dialogues and exchanges between epistemological fields. Abstraction is an activity that involves a vertical reorganization of material and immaterial constructs (from organizing a room to solving a mathematical problem). Plato described abstraction as a way to find the truth, while Bertrand Russell defined it as achieving goals (Mega et al., 2017). An abstraction process is at the beginning of an object or problem and follows its course to a complex structure of thought (complexity here is close to the meaning of Morin, 2008).

The activity of abstraction can be split into three epistemic actions (related to knowledge development): recognition, structuring, and construction (Dreyfus, 1992). Recognition would be the identification of conceptual structures from past experiences. Structuring (or planning) would be the combination of constructs to achieve an objective that involves strategy, justification, and problem-solving. Construction would be the combination of the two previous steps to compose a new knowledge structure based on the context in which the activity takes place.

Abstraction thus goes beyond a simple exercise to a knowledge construction process. It ensures that themes dealt with in various epistemological fields have an understanding ahead of their theoretical perspective, considering the cultural, social, and economic context in which the exercise is established. The generation of knowledge requires structures that include this abstraction exercise, as individuals start from already acquired knowledge to conceive new ones. According to abstraction models, learners enhance their process in the last consolidation exercise. This requires creative and imaginative skills, which teaches them to see what is considered invisible most of the time—for example, the technology itself.

While the process of abstraction refers to the crossing between the invisible territories of China Miéville's novel, cited by Potter (2017), the construction of the interface between epistemological fields is reflected by the bridges built through this exercise. The interface here can be defined symbolically, moving away from its technical meaning of using devices in education.

The interface can be defined as a nuance from social relationships to electronic instruments and devices—systems (physical or symbolic) that allow interaction between individuals, entities, and devices. Technological advances seem to prioritize making this relationship as natural as possible, as intuitive as possible, without requiring the subject to prepare for each interaction to be performed.

With intuitive interaction, the cognitive load can be allocated to more complex processes such as abstraction and knowledge construction (Johnson, 2001). However, a presumptive dichotomy is established when the study of the interface between the fields of knowledge is contextualized since a relationship that could be natural is structured through tensions. The relevance of these tensions is present in the work of Bourdieu (1986), explaining which fields are present in the social dynamics between individuals with specific dispositions called "habitus."

Naturally, forces of capital distribution operate in knowledge fields, which may be intangible (and invisible). The "habitus" is determined by collective strategies constituted by the tensions between subjects and groups, becoming the ingredient that transforms a group into a field. According to Bourdieu (1986), the structure of a lot is dynamic and is established through a set of interactions that are either conditioned or conditioning. The habitus is both individual and collective and can function as a principle that governs the dynamics of a scientific field (aggregation, disaggregation, tension, agreement, and interaction, Thiry-Cherques, 2006).

The interpretation of fields (spaces with structured positions) as dynamic suggests a limited correspondence between this concept in Bourdieu (1986) and the concept of groups of actants in Latour. Nevertheless, it applies the concept of interface between these bridges built between and within epistemological fields. Therefore, this thesis is based on the reference between the interface of areas of knowledge according to this discussion and the abstraction process that possibly, builds the bridge between communication, education, and digital technologies.

With this background, this research presents three abstraction clusters based on the ten categories exposed earlier: the first cluster is named "Actants Network,"; the second is "Power," and the third is "Instrument,"; and together, these three clusters compose a social-technical model to understand digital education. Each group comprises the categories above that may be redundant among the suggested sets. Under the names "Actants Network," "Power," and "Instrument," these clusters express levels of abstraction in the study of technology and education.

*First Cluster: actants network—
a decentralized perspective of human action,
considering a network of actants based on flat ontology*

#	Composition of First Cluster
1	Digital Technology as a Potential to Solve Education Problems
2	Digital Technology as a Logical Operation
5	Digital Technology as a new Education Paradigm
6	Digital Technology as an Extension of Human Perception
7	Technique as an autonomous entity (Big Data, AI, Blockchain, IoT)
8	Digital Technology under an Ecological Approach
9	Digital Technology as a Distributed Narrative among Actants

Table 3: Categories composing the first cluster.

The first group brings at its core an understanding of digital technology in education that goes beyond its use as a tool or an opportunity for training. It offers a perspective that the teaching field starts aggregating human and non-human actants once systems structures are involved. It can be understood that the factors linked to performance, success, and educational activity may depend on the action of learners and educators as well as algorithms, network architectures, and data.

This group brings together a high complexity (in the sense of associating and aggregating countless actants). Therefore, it is located at a level of abstraction ahead of groups two and three. In addition to the categories mentioned above, while reading the articles, it was possible to detect the following topics of discussion:

1. Conceptual dimensions of digital literacies, media, information, and transliteracies;
2. Digital technologies and quality of higher education;

3. Philosophy of technique; and
4. Applications of digital technology in the educational sphere.

In the case of the topics mentioned above, they cohabit with the first group and the categories. It can be inferred that it was during the writing of the discussions that the conclusion was reached as to which categories would make up this particular group.

Beginning with the dimensions of digital literacies, literacy can be defined as the ability to lead one's own life, read and write sufficiently to communicate well with society and do logical operations, not just arithmetic. It can be defined as a broad term that reflects a society's need for information, recognizing that the definition of an individual developed in their literacies changes according to the use and appropriation of information resources and packages. Therefore, the interface of literacy with media, information, and digital technology consist of performances both on the individual and on the part of technical systems.

Here appears to be the core of the transdisciplinary structure of the term. The prefix "trans" is an organizational characteristic that affects how different media interact and establish new aggregations (Castells & Illera, 2018). It also influences the context in which teaching occurs, as it has at its core the questioning of the categorical divisions of knowledge established by traditional school education. The "trans" involves understanding a non-linear narrative of the learning and content production processes. This capacity becomes a demand for learners, educators, and technical systems.

To understand the applicability of the concept of literacy, the structure of the term implies that learners should exercise their full potential. Nevertheless, contemporary digital technology requires an ecology of literacies (comprising different types of skills). Being developed in multiple literacies in the 21st century involves decoding and understanding multimodal texts and digital formats and purposefully engaging with these texts. Literacy is not based on specific skills; instead, it is the process of amalgamating digital technology's social and collaborative dynamics.

Yet, it seems interesting to reframe the concept of information literacy as a metaliteracy (supporting multiple types of literacies) due to the growth of online communities (Ungerer, 2016). Information literacy involves more than a discrete set of skills, making metaliteracy a comprehensive framework encompassing other types of literacies and their connections. It serves as the foundation for: media, digital, information, communication, technology, and visual literacy—as the great paradigm of education in the digital economy of the 21st century is the creation and promotion of a wide range of skills.

Unlike teaching in the 20th century (when reading a text was a sedimented method of accessing information for learning), teaching learners about mastery of technology, media, and information skills requires the emphasis on a multimodal approach, as the Internet's multimodal delivery system provides opportunities for the simulation and use of various types of stimuli. Discussions about the multimodal method argue that socio-technical networks can capture data beyond textual responses or video, opening an opportunity for AI application.

In this debate, it is common to focus on digital technologies and the quality of higher education, positioning university education as a significant consumer of innovative technologies and the backbone of the digital economy that fosters new employment possibilities. Yet, despite technological innovation being designed to equate to the nature of the educational process, it has the challenge of overcoming traditional and rigid teaching standards, which treat innovation only as a means to an end. Innovation must be relevant to curricular and learning goals, promoting logical principles and digital interaction, which correlates with critical thinking and the role of technology in education.

Critical thinking refers to literacies in three categories: ideological representation, positioning, and production. But first, it seems interesting to rely on the perspective of Heidegger (1986) to question what technique is. Heidegger's ideas are tied to the etymological meaning of words without delving into human beings' development. Heidegger examines technological development and its distance from the essence of the human being, establishing the following conceptual distinctions: technique as a means to an end and technique as a human act. Both conceptions of technique are correlated, reaffirming its instrumental vision. Instead, a broader understanding of technique might be auxiliary in understanding its proper role in education.

Oliveira and Giacomazzo (2018) find four primary meanings of technology:

1. The first is technology as theory, science, study, and discussion of technique—a necessary purpose to understand other classifications;
2. The second meaning is the technology equivalent to technique since the two words are used recurrently to express both one and the other, revealing the possible confusion generated by this equivalence of meanings in the judgment of philosophical and sociological problems. This matching of terms, however, does not occur by chance. The use of technology terminology, as the authors justify, enhances the technical activity and establishes connections with the ideologies of interest of dominant groups or nations (tech coloniality);
3. As a third meaning, technology can be understood as the set of all the techniques of society at any historical stage of its development. The understanding is that the term is closely linked to the previous meaning: technology equivalent to technique. Therefore, when comparing the evolution of technology in each historical period, reference is made to this third meaning of technology; and
4. Fourth, technology can be defined as an ideology: by alienating oneself, the working man does not perceive himself as a transforming agent of society. The concept of technology is constantly under construction, and humans often look at the product of the technique. They do not feel capable of doing it, not realizing the capacity to build such a feat and enable themselves to do so.

Supposedly, technological development, which in the service of capitalism needs to produce greater volume and speed, creates a mechanism that prevents man from thinking critically. Therefore, literacies could be seen as an analytical, reflective, and evaluative attitude of the subject's information through ICTs. Buckingham (2010) clarifies that the goal of digital literacy is not to develop technical skills. Furthermore, it encourages a global understanding of how technologies work and promotes ways of thinking about their uses.

By citing the debate on technique and its approach to the concept of technology, it is possible to approach the perceptions of Bateson (1987) and

Simondon (2017) on technique to think about technologies in education. Both Bateson (1987) and Simondon (2005) were trained in transdisciplinary areas and therefore did not identify with the definitions of the technique arising from static fields of knowledge. According to Simondon (2005), new tech culture is necessary for four reasons:

1. Because the information coming from the machines only raises meanings within a specific technical culture;
2. The need for a technically illustrated culture as a way of emancipation;
3. By considering the genesis and evolution of technical beings within a given cultural framework; and
4. Due to the insufficiency of evaluations in strictly technical terms, the technique culture must inspire humility in the face of the integrity of the whole.

Simondon (2005) understands technology as a second-degree technique in organizing these rational points. For this reason, it allows recognizing the creation of essence and avoiding alienation when using a technical object without knowing its origin and capabilities. In Bateson (1987) and Simondon (2017), conditions of technicality refer to internal and external environment integration in adaptation processes.

For both, the responsibility of the technique relates to integrating it and making it compatible with the information one inhabits. Bateson (1987) and Simondon (2017) contributed to this cybernetic vision where both organisms and their environments are understood as interacting message systems. The idea of civilization, which arises from the ecology of mind proposed by Bateson (1987), can give positive content to the new culture of technique claimed by Simondon (2017).

After this brief discussion on the first cluster, one question remains: is it talking about a new paradigm in education? Pavlik (2015) talks about a possible third paradigm in which technology exerts at least four influences on education: the transformation of teaching and learning methods; reformulation of the content of what is taught and learned; transformation of educational institutions, structures, and costs; and redefining relationships between students and educators.

Early digital developments in the 1990s influenced one, two, or three of these areas. However, the four topics need to be transformed for a paradigm shift. Pavlik (2015) relies on Kuhn (2013), who noted in his work that the paradigmatic transition involves changing basic concepts that underpin a discipline or field of knowledge.

The new logic of knowledge production at the interface with a range of hybrid methodological procedures can give rise to the third paradigm of education. Reminding the history of these three paradigms, the first has existed for thousands of years and operated in a pre-technological era: the one-on-one tutoring and mentoring format. The second emerged with the advent of analog media, especially with books printed in the middle ages, a one-to-many teaching model. This model is less effective than direct mentoring, as the mentees' response process is more subjective.

Education could be at the dawn of its third paradigm, especially with the technological and behavioral advances due to the COVID-19 pandemic, which is defined by the connection between students and teachers and the characteristics of many-to-many and multi-directional mentoring. The teacher no longer holds the great master of knowledge role: they are mentors or guides, and students engage in the process of sharing knowledge and exploring discovery.

This paradigm represents the decline of the teaching hierarchy, the end of courses when teaching becomes barrier-free and disciplines can communicate. Learning is a mutual exploration and discovery process between students and people formerly recognized as teachers. The arrival of the third paradigm does not condemn the end of the other two, just as the appearance of the second did not expel the first. However, they are set aside insofar as they are still considered necessary.

Second Cluster: power—perspective promoting power balance focused on skills development and human centrality

#	Composition of Second Cluster
1	Digital Technology as a Potential to Solve Education Problems
2	Digital Technology as a Logical Operation
4	Digital Technology as a New Paradigm of Post-Modern Societies
5	Digital Technology as a new Education Paradigm
6	Digital Technology as an Extension of Human Perception
9	Digital Technology as a Distributed Narrative among Actants
10	Digital Technology as a Humanocentric Narrative

Table 4: Categories composing the second cluster.

The second abstraction cluster suggests that digital technology aims to empower the human actant in the field of education. This group supports the perspective that the learner and the educator apply digital technology and, consequently, expand in this process, bringing new horizons to their users. The categories listed above compile the definitions and ideas of the present cluster.

However, in contrast to the first group presented in the previous section, this set offers a particular centrality to the human figure, transforming digital technology into something that can be mastered. Even to master the technology, the human becomes influenced by its use. According to theorists such as Marshall McLuhan, it could represent an extension (or massage) of the human senses toward the dominated technology. As much as this extension may suggest that technology eventually dominates human action (as argued by Heidegger), there is still a particular centrality and protagonism of human activity over digital technology. The doubt about the only centrality of the action between the interface between digital technology, communication, and education can be presented when data and algorithms seem to exert influence in digital social networks or digital pedagogical activities.

Unlike the first cluster, with multiple discussion topics, this group presents only one central issue discussed by the analyzed articles: digital technologies and teacher education. Digital competence can be described as skills and attitudes towards digital media and information for work, entertainment, and study purposes. As part of the curriculum, developing digital literacy addresses the changing nature of subject knowledge, recognizing that young people need different skills, knowledge, and understanding to develop their expertise. Digital literacy enables young people to be competent, efficient, and critical in the Digital Age. When implemented in the curriculum, it opens doors to other types of literacies with interchangeable and connective skills.

Third Cluster: instrument – instrumentalist perspective focused on human centrality

#	Composition of Second Cluster
1	Digital Technology as a Potential to Solve Education Problems
3	Digital Technology as a Tool
4	Digital Technology as a New Paradigm of Post-Modern Societies
10	Digital Technology as a Humanocentric Narrative

Table 5: Categories composing the third cluster.

The third cluster has as its main characteristic the use of digital technology as a tool in communication and education. A perspective supports this characteristic that digital technology (or technique) is an instrument or a means to an end.

As discussed in previous chapters, the instrumentalist conception of technology has an Aristotelian foundation when the philosopher separates thought (episteme) from technique (tekne). During the history of technological evolution, inventions may have been used as tools at first. However, in addition to enabling the execution of specific tasks, technology has changed the human inhabit in terms of size and even potential. For example, inventions such as the wheel and the steam engine were intended to take human beings from point A to point B, but they changed the geographical dimension of human habitation.

Examples of technological developments can conclude that thinking of technology only as a tool may be insufficient. Suppose technology is thought of as a means to an end. In that case, it is prudent to recognize that it is not known what end is intended to be achieved or the dimension of the result to be acquired (the second world war and the advent of the atomic bomb can demonstrate that).

However, the instrumentalist perspective is not dispensable, and its application becomes understandable, especially in the educational context. In education, the technical structures of digital artifacts can be challenging to understand in their functioning. This can lead educators and learners to reserve themselves from not understanding it in-depth, appropriating it only as a tool.

As much as the internet is considered an expansion of possibilities, technologies are often seen as fundamental tools for the teaching-learning process. As a result, digital literacy can be defined as a series of socially and culturally situated values, practices, and skills involved in operating linguistically within electronic environments, including reading, writing, and communication.

It is interesting here to propose a detachment of the concept of "education" from the idea of "school" based on Morin to defend a multidimensional education based on the principle of complexity. Complexity in education enables the discussion of new dialogic structures and network dynamics. Educational transformations link opportunities for interaction with information, which could mean a new paradigm of knowledge.

After reviewing the three clusters, this chapter aimed to present how the studies of digital education have the potential to convey tech more than just learning solutions. Starting from an essay that explores the theoretical depth of Big Data, the platformization phenomenon, Artificial Intelligence, and Blockchain, this chapter presents a conceptual contribution to how digital technologies develop dynamics between humans and non-humans. These dynamics can intuit that the digital leaves its instrumental dimension as a means to an end, becoming an extension of the human being and qualitatively altering how a sphere composed of several entities is inhabited.

During the argument about the qualitative change brought about by digital technologies on the human gaze in the living environment itself, this work elaborated ten theoretical categories on how digital technologies are understood, studied and explained in education. After exposing and deepening the categories, they were grouped into three abstraction clusters (actants network, power, and instrument). The subsequent sessions will address how these three clusters can compose a social-technical model, the SETA model, in which education technology can be analyzed in a layered architecture.

Chapter 3

Developing a Conceptual Model

In the previous chapters, ten categories that explain digital education attempted to describe how tech can and is applied to learning. Consequently, these categories were grouped into three abstraction clusters that will now be managed into a social-technical model. As previously explained, the exercise of abstraction expands the potential of understanding the study and application of digital technology in education. With this in mind, it is considered that the three abstraction clusters can compose a social-technical model to understand the operation of this interface. It is important to say that it is relevant that the model passes through the contemplation of the three clusters so that conceptual and practical aspects of the interface between digital technology and education can be addressed.

But first, it seems reasonable to understand conceptual models and how they flirt with social-technical studies. Conceptual models can be defined as abstract representations of aspects of reality. It is not by chance that when the learner is approached, the "educational model of tutoring" or the "educational model of one to many" are mentioned, which establishes conceptual standards in which it is possible to comprehend the reference to private or classroom tutoring.

Morin (1986) explores conceptual models in an attempt to understand how knowledge is processed in the human brain through a trajectory that the author names "knowing knowledge" that begins with the question: "is it possible to know knowledge?". In the search for meta-knowledge, Morin resorts to models that tend to explain the relationship between mind, knowledge, brain, and subjectivity. For Morin, knowledge is a multidimensional, physical, biological, cerebral, mental, psychological, cultural, and social phenomenon that has been "cracked" within the culture. Western society, by the organization of knowledge itself, especially by the disjunction between science and philosophy and by the disciplinary fragmentation of science, culminated in the crisis of the idea of foundation in philosophy.

To circumvent the disciplinary division that, according to Morin, is an obstacle in meta-knowledge, he resorts to chemical, biological, philosophical, physical, and social models to find a universal pattern of how knowledge occurs. He observes, however, that in the face of the numerous models analyzed, there is one constant: the scientific movement of paradigm shift. Recalling Kuhn (2013), paradigms are conventions and standards defined within the scope of research groups that govern the scientific area of specific disciplines. Conceptual models (in which they try to explain observed phenomena) are correlated with these conventions and, by a natural evolution of science, are questioned and eventually broken to follow new research and subsequent models.

Moments of a paradigmatic rupture usually constitute a general crisis of perception. The instruments used to understand reality no longer serve to capture the necessary information and become inadequate to describe the turbulence of a world in permanent transformation. To go ahead with the task of knowing knowledge, Morin proposes to start from the contribution of knowledge brought by both Gödel's theorem and Tarski's logic, which offer, in short, that no cognitive system would be able to know itself exhaustively, nor to validate themselves thoroughly, based on their instruments of knowledge. This does not mean giving up on achieving meta-knowledge but understanding that incompleteness and living with blind spots is a condition of knowledge.

Morin's quest to understand models leads him to conclude that universal models are flawed and must be contextualized or localized to make sense. Still, he emphasizes how good the elaboration of conceptual models is, pointing out that this practice is justified when attached to the commitment to study one set of actants in-depth, which is approached in the disciplinary interface. A way to facilitate this dialogue about conceptual models is to use the example of a car. When the word "car" is spoken, the mind understands that it is a four-wheel structure capable of moving itself.

Still, the image of a structure commanded by an engine and fuel on round wheels is printed—a model suitable for cars on flat roads, which requires the displacement of the structure. One does not think of square wheels when one thinks of a car, as their mobility would be compromised on flat terrain.

However, if the vehicle were designed to go up and downstairs, perhaps "non-round wheels" would be more appropriate. What this example tries to convey is that conceptual models are mental structures dependent on contextualization and abstraction. The application of models to build vehicles or knowledge structures depends on the potential contextualization and abstraction that a context may or may not offer.

Therefore, the discussion around conceptual models is tied to interface definitions and contextualization of local environments of application. The conceptual model of the three abstraction clusters aims to instill in the analysis of theoretical studies and project three praxis phases of education technology. Promoting a qualitative approach, this model seeks to sponsor: content (subjective knowledge, support, and supervision of data analytics); delivery (quality, pace, and accuracy); and recognition (assessment, accreditation, and validation). And for that, the model proposes a layered systemic model based on computational development. Studies of the implementation of networks among computer systems, after decades (since 1946 with the first Electronic Numerical Integrator and Computer—ENIAC) of research and tests, are today based on the universal model of computer interface networks based on layers.

Computer communications are performed through channels made available by a provider layer (also known as a driver or bus) that offers an environment consisting of a series of services and resources that enables the message to be sent. This provider layer behaves like a logical driver capable of interconnecting the various actants. Above the driver are peered layers in which each one performs a service that enables the transmission of information. For instance, there are some requirements in naming peered layers: they must be at the same distance from the driver and pair their functions. Each layer performs a service type for the layer above, and each layer (after its job/function) provides a service package for the subsequent layer.

Each layer thus has an access point to these services performed so that the layer above can take advantage of the work (what in computing is called a Service Access Point [SAP]) and then develop the rest of the work. When the last layer accesses this SAP, it applies a protocol (an algorithm fed by Protocol Data Unit [PDU]) to translate the service provided into actions that this last layer needs to perform. From there, the layer uses its services to complete its work. When the layer works, it generates a new package and a new SAP, and the cycle repeats. The image below explains what this cycle and diagram format would be:

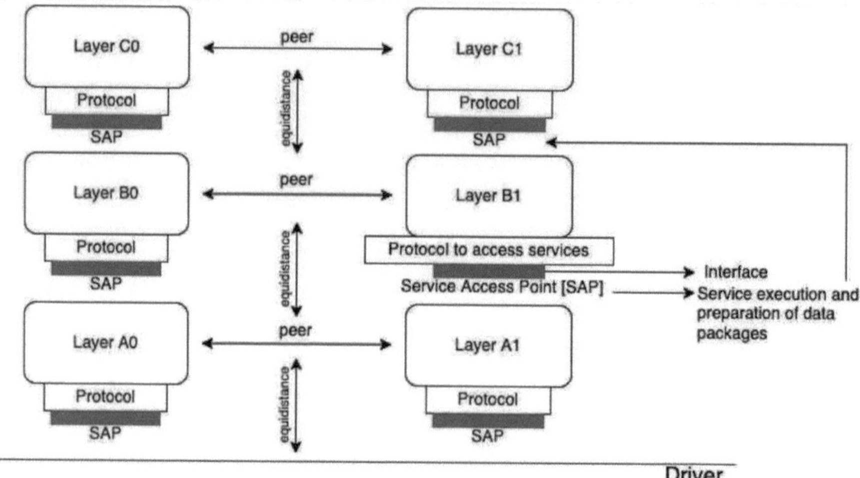

Figure 3: Computational universal model. Source: Author, 2022.

This complex and mouthfull scheme can be understood by illustrating human verbal communication. When translated into human communication, the example of systems communication has some weaknesses, such as the fact that the individual is a subjective actant, the language has linguistic variables, and emotions and cultural artifacts are involved in the communicative process. However, this example is used to understand how this systemic structuring occurs since all human beings communicate at some level.

This may seem a bit abstract, but when observing the barring of verbal communication between two people: humans communicate (when in person and considering that they have no impediment of speaking and listening skills) through sound, which has a specific means of propagation: the air (more specifically the earth's atmosphere). Therefore, the terrestrial atmosphere works as the driver to provide an ecosystem where communication occurs. The language here assumes the role of a layer with an SAP, as languages have their lexical and syntactic rules. Also, the human hearing and speaking organs and systems are a layer with SAP since they have their specificities. In the case of two human individuals communicating, when they don't understand the language, they don't need to change layers related to their physical ability to hear or speak (assuming they don't have any impairment involved); they could try only to change the layer of communication—employing another language, for example.

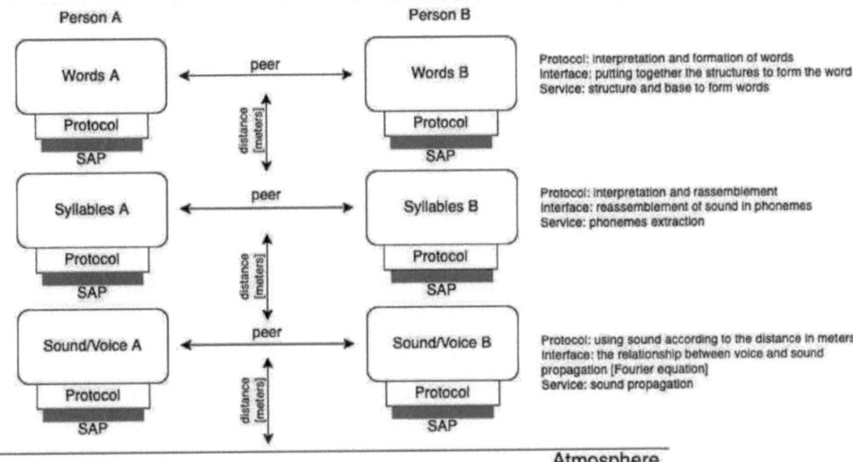

Figure 4: Computational model applied to verbal communication. Source: Author, 2022.

In the case of the digital network, the Internet plays the role of a universal driver through which global stakeholders can communicate. The internet allows an equidistance of actants who communicate, allowing them to exchange and share information regardless of location. Yet, it is worth saying that this layered system is employed in this research for two reasons:

1. If one layer of communication is not suitable or not working well, there's no need to change the entire model or system: all it takes is to change the layer. As demonstrated in the human communication example before, the same happens with computers: when there is a problem with the screen of a device, there is no need to change the entire machine or its operational system: it is enough to change the setting and structure of the screen; and

2. Two, because this model allows the applicant to check the communication requirements on the receiving end. This means, for example, if one tries to employ an educational technology in a

particular population group at a school, they have to have a common driver for this partnership to work—not only regarding internet connections but also looking at tech needs, cultural understanding of devices and other more abstract aspects. And this is the logic behind the peered layer: they must be on the same level of experience to communicate. Otherwise, the system fails.

Yet, there is no presumption here to establish a theory or communication system. This work aims to understand how the three clusters can compose a framework for analyzing educational technology projects or curricula.

Social Technical Model for Education Technology Application [SETA]

The acronym SETA harvests its meaning in the Portuguese word "seta," which means "arrow." An arrow figure has two different implications in this book: to point exact directions and—to reference Latour—to remind the unmerciless "arrow of time" that brings humanity the post-modernity. It is a tool to tailor products to targeted groups but also an environment to nurture the reasoning about the present and future possibilities regarding technology development. This is why on the cover of the book there is a picture of the Greek Goddess Artemis, the Goddess of the hunt, to symbolize the human hunt for knowledge and the arrow to symbolize the SETA model.

As discussed before, the exercise of crossing barriers between fields of knowledge is what this work defines as an abstraction. The interface becomes the bridge built through the process of abstraction, enabling dialogues and exchanges between epistemological fields. Remembering, abstraction is an activity that involves a vertical reorganization of material and immaterial constructs (from organizing a room to solving a mathematical problem). This process occurs at the beginning of an object or situation and proceeds toward a complex thinking structure. Therefore, this research is based on the interface between knowledge areas and the abstraction process that possibly, builds the bridge between communication, education, and digital technologies.

In the previous section, there is a description of how the computer network model functions through layer interaction generating network communication. In this section, an appropriation of this structure is attempted to represent the clusters (actant network, power, and instrument), how they are related and how they can function as layers. SETA is divided into layers because if there is a malfunction, it is unnecessary to replace the entire system, only the corresponding layer, suggesting that the layering scheme implies their codependence and interchangeability.

This dynamic relationship between layers is similar to the clusters: they are interchangeable, codependent, and based on common drivers. However, models can be flawed and must be contextualized to make sense. It is prudent to emphasize the commitment to study the set of actants in-depth, addressed in the disciplinary interface. A conceptual model could serve as a compass to understand this interface. A common driver offers the conditions and requirements of a system to operate the underlying layers.

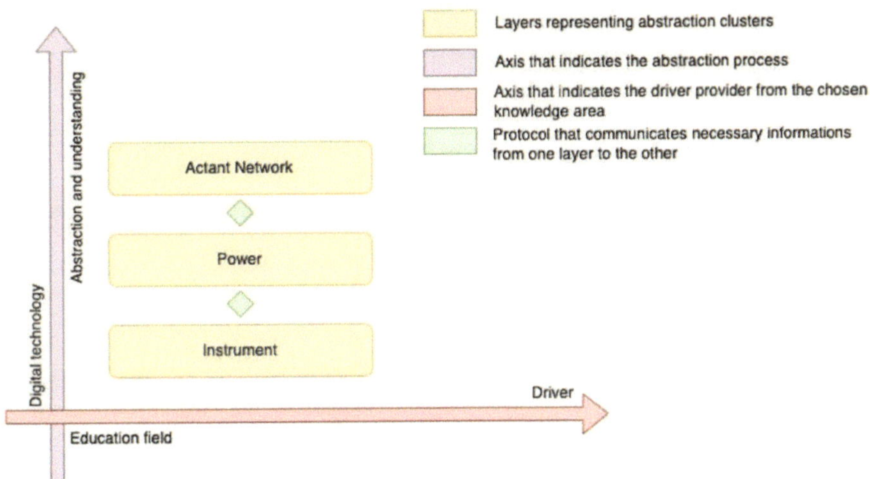

Figure 5: SETA model. Source: Author, 2022.

In the present proposal, the driver works, offering conditions and requirements of a knowledge area to understand digital technologies and their potential contributions in a given disciplinary field (education). Perpendicular to the driver, it is possible to establish a vertical axis called "understanding and abstraction." When in layers, the groups will be arranged according to their existence on a common driver and will vary their level according to the perceptions and comprehension on the base of the "understanding and abstraction" axis.

The layers are also responsive, being possible to rearrange them according to the common interpretation of a group of what technology is and how it can be applied. If it is not being applied to education but among a group of experts in Information Philosophy, then maybe the closer layer to them will be the more abstract and philosophical one: actant network.

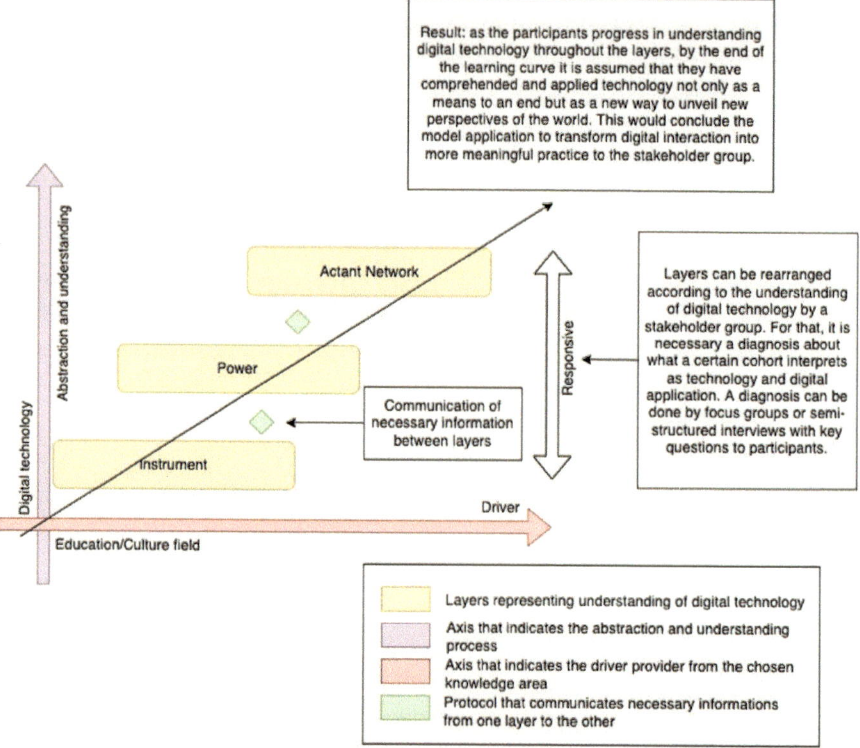

Figure 6: SETA model responsiveness. Source: Author, 2022.

For example, in a project to develop digital solutions for a school in a specific location, the model offers a previous analysis of the current understanding of technology based on participants' location and cultural background. Here the digital solution could be co-created meaningfully, having the group's definitions and conceptions of technology as a base.

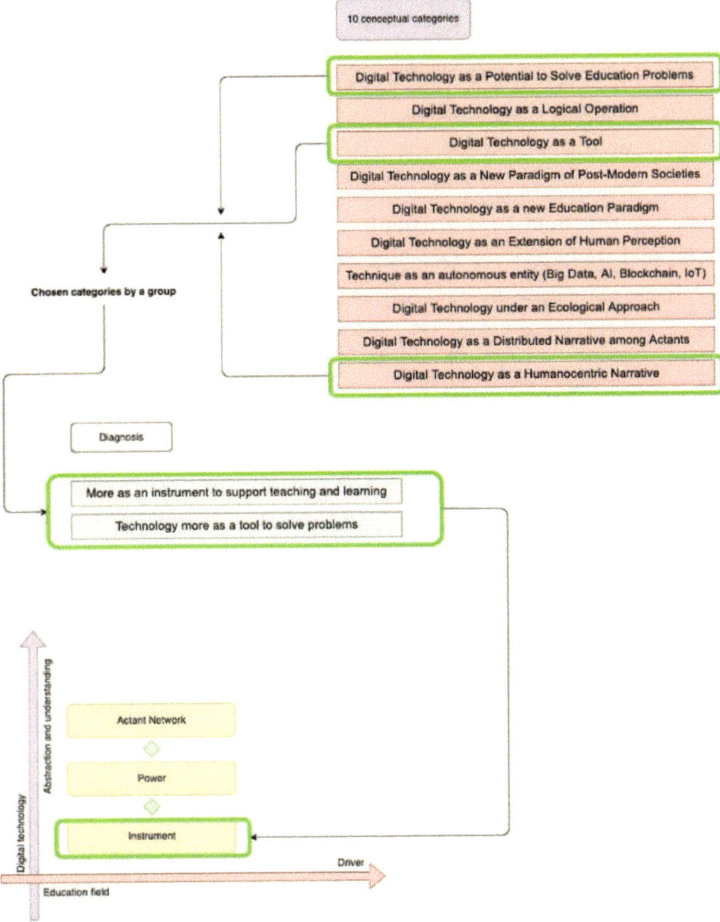

Figure 7: SETA model appliance. Source: Author, 2022.

If, in this hypothetical scenario, the set of actants understand technology more as a tool to solve problems or more as an instrument to support teaching and learning, then in the model, the layer closer to the common driver is the layer of "instrument." It will be possible to discuss and debate the other two sides of the technology interface: power and actant network. With this in mind, this model aims to establish which of the three abstraction clusters is closer to one's understanding of technology to build a common comprehension of how technology can be meaningfully interfaced with education.

When in layers, the groups simulate the existence of protocols. They must provide base information to the upper layers to be sufficiently understood. Therefore, there is the existence of these protocols presenting critical topics for understanding digital technologies.

However, this conceptual social-technical model is responsive in reorganizing the layers referring to specific fields of knowledge, as seen in the model, when considering the field of information philosophy as a driver. It is possible to observe that the layers are reorganized, keeping close to the group's driver with the highest correlation to the conceptions and opinions about digital technology in the area of knowledge. Therefore, the model has as a requirement the execution of a knowledge area diagnosis, incorporating the following steps:

1. Selection of the knowledge area;
2. Selection of a group of actants over which this model will be applied;
3. Diagnosis of theoretical concepts about digital technology among the chosen group;
4. Diagnosis of which of the ten categories are closest to the group's conceptions and by which abstraction group begins the study of digital technology; and
5. Assembly of the conceptual model.

The model's purpose is to be a compass to guide the approach of digital technologies by the three abstraction groups since this work argues that for a holistic understanding of digital technologies, it would be relevant to go through the three abstraction groups in layered forms. The three aspects go together: the consideration of digital technology as a network of human and non-human actants; digital technology as an extension of human perception that leads to the achievement of potentialities and power; and as a tool or a means to an end and to accomplish tasks—the layers guide which strands to start to achieve the extensive abstraction exercise.

SETA model's first validation

Since this model was first created in 2020, it had a few chances to be validated and adequately tested. This section will bring details of testing done at the heart of the indigenous territories in Amazonia/Brazil. As of March 11th, 2020, the world has been declared under the COVID-19 pandemic—which meant that countries were underneath sanitary restrictions that included (to name a phew): physical/social distancing, lockdowns, and mask-wearing. The world resourced its activities online, several work sectors applied home office regimes, and the economy suffered a particular hit with this paradigm change: the mandatory transition from presencial to virtual life.

Some sectors suffered even a more substantial hit, for example, education and social services, in which digital inclusion gaps became wider, shedding light on how unfair is digital access around the world. However, what seemed to be a challenge was also a chance for creativity. Local community groups started to co-create solutions that could solve the problems imposed by the pandemic.

In the case of Brazilian Amazonia, more specifically in the South West region of the forest, they faced a set of specific challenges: with the river navigation suspended by local government, supplies had difficulty reaching isolated communities—including food, clean water, medicines, and hygiene products. In addition, in June 2020, little was known about the pandemic, and even less in these populational settings. Therefore, they resourced to make a campaign to bring both food/ hygiene supplies and information to fifteen indigenous settlements.

The native territories also tried to protect themselves by closing their entrances while asking for help to ward off prospectors and land grabbers. Amazonian ethnicities, therefore, made barricades to control the entry and exit of people. Parallel to the barriers, groups organized digital networks gathering strategic informational possibilities for native peoples, including translating the sanitary regulations from the Portuguese language to indigenous dialects. In this process, it became somewhat clear that Amerindian groups have been going through a complex digital transformation mode, which involves the use of devices and connections between ethnicities. The pandemic brought densification of these networks. It is the digitization of lands, people, and things.

This "info materialization" recalls, for example, the Krahô ethnicity's ability to transmit funeral rites on TV or social networks for those who could not follow closely due to social distancing. In addition to rituals, ethnicities were connected through different instruments and tools for transmitting knowledge to foster exchange and trade networks in shamanic and resistance connections.

Through these instruments and methods, experiences have been shared, invasions filmed, and violence cases reported. Much of this is published daily on communication networks alongside tactical information about COVID-19. As a particular highlight, the Wayuri network in the Alto Rio Negro region periodically records podcasts about the epidemic outbreak, revealing ways to prevent and combat the spread of the virus in the territories.

These existing "info materialization" structures were then employed to solve the lack of food/hygiene supplies and trustworthy information translated into native dialects and is precisely to solve the second problem that the SETA model was applied. After the pandemic decree, social networks began demonstrating a series of content on fighting the virus and dealing with mass social isolation.

At the same time, the word "vertiginous" was employed to describe the amount of information, a phenomenon called infodemic—a pandemic of data—as defined by the World Health Organization. The challenge of infodemic is not only the amount but the quality and veracity of information circulating, which requires from the audience a critical oversight of this available contents, and an education process to develop essential skills among citizens, so they are skilled to evaluate information's quantity and quality.

With selecting, translating, and making available, trustworthy information about the SARS-COV-2—comes the job of developing skills among the fifteen populational groups and their respective indigenous dialects. But here resides the question: how to establish an ordinary start in which these groups could express their understanding of the situation and, from there, develop an educational process through digital technologies to understand the pandemic status and gravity better? The SETA model could do that.

As explained before, in general terms, communication operates on a driver (provider layer), configured by an environment that provides a series of services and items that enable the issuance of messages. Above the driver, there are even layers, and each one performs a type of service, making it possible to transmit information. Each layer, after the driver, conducts a kind of service for the layer above through the emission of a service package.

However, when revising this social-technical model, one question remains: what is the common driver between the solutions to the problems and the populational groups that identified the issues? It cannot be the atmosphere, as they are not in the exact location or geography. It cannot be solely the internet, as there is no ubiquity of access between communication ends. It is then up to the different groups to build a common driver.

The construction of a common driver to communicate through reliable information between public or private agents and vulnerable communities would not happen automatically (under a pre-existing structure) or universally (which could serve for all situations dissemination of information). The drive would then take place in the sum of a few steps, namely:

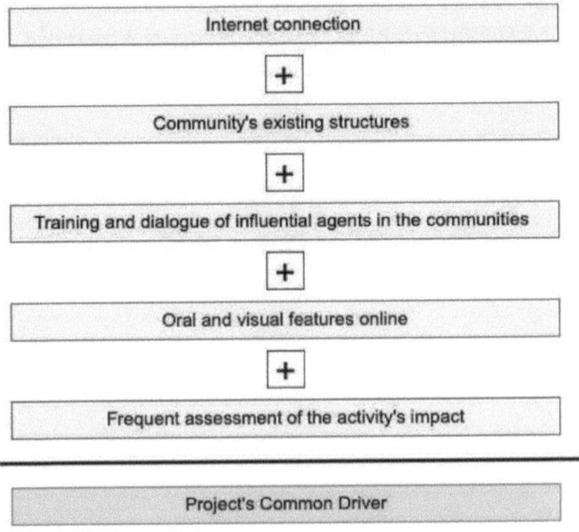

Figure 8: Project's common provider. Source: Author, 2022.

It is important to note that orality in communities carries within themselves the knowledge that inhabits the body and is expressed through telling or narrating stories (Bairon, 2004). However, western philosophy typically cancels these narratives by ignoring these voices in scientific writing, not assuming these constructions of dialogue as "science" or assuming them as "pseudoscience." However, diversity of knowledge development is amidst an entire native creation. With this driver in mind, a video production network was launched with the Federal University of Amazonas. Linguistic and culturally translated information became the weapon to fight the virus. The communities became the central authorship in making such essential information resources and the educational process. All videos were designed in co-authorship with the communities' teachers, leaders, political entities, and collaborators.

Once the common driver was understood, it was time to diagnose which of the three abstraction clusters was closer to the populational groups. For that, focal groups took place showcasing local influencers to comprehend how they saw and applied technology and informational resources. When asked, the fifteen different groups described technology and informational resources as "Potential to Solve Education and Quotidien Problems," as a "New Paradigm of Post-Modern Societies," as an "Extension of Human Perception" and as a "Human Narrative," which puts them closer to the cluster "Power." After they described technology as a communication tool, placing it as a second cluster "Instrument" and, finally, the most distant and philosophical one, "Actant Network."

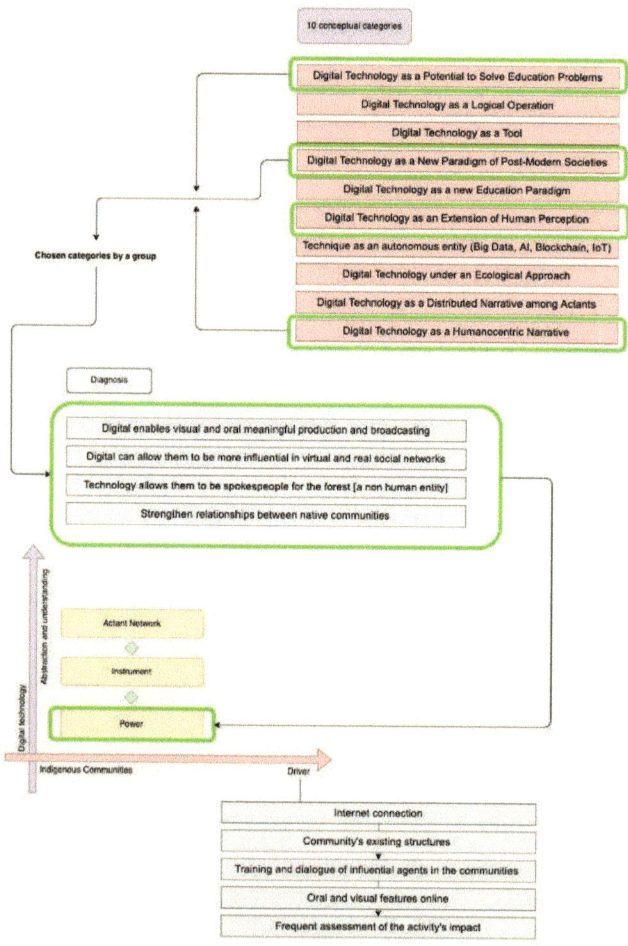

Figure 9: SETA model validation. Source: Author, 2022.

They have then described how technology boosts their oral and visual production, which are meaningful ways of communicating among themselves. Some groups have also expressed the intention of becoming more digitally influential and to be spokespersons for the forest [which is interesting since they put themselves as spokesperson for a non-human entity—implying that the non-human entity has demands of itself that need to be addressed politically]. Some of them also described that digital strengthens the relationships between communities. They can communicate and share experiences and solutions to challenges [something hard to be done before digital connection].

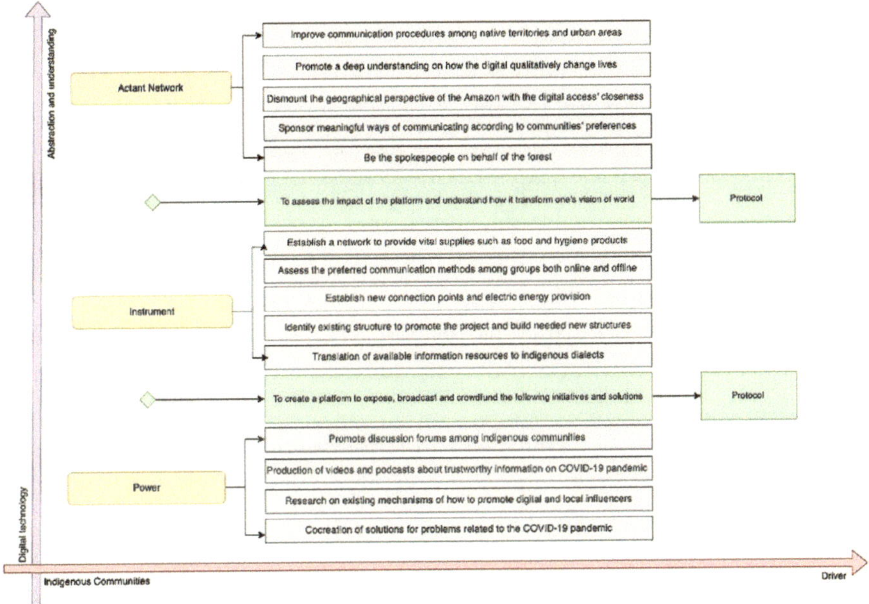

Figure 10: SETA model assessment. Source: Author, 2022.

Naturally, with the focus groups, many answers were compiled so that every community would have its specific drivers, layers, and SETA model applications. However, collected data were analyzed through NVivo to understand the pattern under which a project like this would be able to properly develop solutions that would be meaningful for all the fifteen communities and their respective languages. Translations of videos, audios, and texts were performed in Munduruku, Sateré-Mawé, Ticuna, and Tenharim dialects, among others.

Together with the indigenous territories, the goal was to break the disinformation cycle and counter-information about COVID-19, acting through collaborative tactics focused on the specificities of the Amazon region. In this sense, populations have appropriated technologies to help their communities. As a result, they could co-create solutions in meaningful ways to avoid the spread of COVID-19, improving their skills in assessing information and digital curation and production. In that sense, the SETA model seems to have excelled in this process, bringing together the essential topics to be addressed by the communities and the project's goals.

In exploring this validation experience, this book proposes a first step in building a model and admits that future applications and experiences can ensure its improvement. Floridi (2014) highlights that e-education (as he calls it) is linked to knowledge and, as the information society witnesses the challenging growth of data. Therefore, there is a demand to understand the structures behind the learning processes. According to Floridi, cognitive learning architectures are similar to the logic of algorithms, which is why these processes should provide dialogues between their fields. The basic structure of education must be such as to unite knowledge architecture, incipience, uncertainty, and naivety, and the real question is not "how" to teach the next generation, but "what."

Future e-education appears to cross the boundaries of categories of mind and follow a transdisciplinary path to realize a complex understanding of the surrounding world. As Floridi (2014) mentions, "science changes our understanding in two fundamental ways: about the world and ourselves" (p. 87). Science compiled with education can be the key to understanding how abstraction clusters are developed within digital perspectives.

The challenge of carrying out research in this field is to align academic elaborations (such as this) with the pragmatic context (primary, secondary schools, and other educational levels). In addition, to enable the population and government to understand the implications of what appears to be a new possibility for knowledge philosophy and, if not yet a new paradigm, a vision of a changing reality in how humanity is learning.

Final Uncertainties

Dealing with the Invisible

This book understands that, in recent years, theories and writers, disciplines, and parallel perspectives occupy the same spaces as in the work of Miéville (2010)—as narrated by Potter (2017). Sometimes, such fields build and develop empires of knowledge while avoiding recognizing this co-presence, a procedure that can be naturalized in the scientific structure. This phenomenon seems to be the imposition of barriers that make related fields incommunicable. This is precisely the problem of demarcation that Popper (1987) addressed (explained in the Prologue) and why education technology should create bridges so knowledge realms can co-exist while acknowledging one-another existences.

Crossing the barriers between fields/demarcations is called an abstraction exercise. In developing this work, it was observed that digital technology could be associated with radical forms of change, and "disruptive education" can describe a phenomenon of using common technologies to address the emerging values of both learners and educators.

Disruption, as a concept synonymous with the idea of a turning point, is justified by efforts that support digital education superficially, touching the inefficiencies of the educational status quo. Instead of a technicist idea of digital education, a comprehensive approach to human sensitivities about devices and networks could offer a new way of thinking about education technology. Perhaps, true disruption is not about using technology to do the same things differently but to do fundamentally different things (Selwyn, 2016).

Education technology is seen as the level of change, celebrated as a set of initiatives that improve educational success. This relationship in improving learning or teaching often prescribes digital technology in a sequence of verbs in which systems enable, assist, assess, and support learning. However, as Selwyn (2016) argues, other levels of change are contemplated around digital technologies when associated with transforming educational processes and practices as a reference to the renewal and revolution of the nature and forms of education. This shift seems to imply a series of methodological and philosophical transitions. It suggests that digital technologies lead education processes—assuming a blow to the established order, associating technological approaches with scientific paradigm shifts (as discussed in the Prologue). Nevertheless, the disruptive innovation thesis offers an inconvenient truth that there may be no real benefit to digital education, shedding light on the possibility that learning settings don't need new tools but new mindsets to reinvent education for the future.

Therefore, arguments that digital technology is a repair of the educational system are outdated. The interface between digital learning is a complex process, and digital solutions in education can be accompanied by circuits for the sale and purchase of ideas, equipment, and projects—distancing technological sufficiency so that the market remains in constant progress. Suddenly, the need for digital devices seems to speak louder than education itself, to the point that innovation in education can lose its meaning altogether.

Yet, it is unfair to assume that technology is simply pointless, and this book recognizes that the digital offers a qualitatively different experience of habiting the 21st Century. The complexity of this interface also seems to permeate the interactions between knowledge and science. In searching for answers to these epistemological relationships, Morin (1986) resorts to models that explain the relationship between mind, knowledge, brain, and subjectivity. For Morin, knowledge is a multidimensional phenomenon, simultaneously physical, biological, cerebral, mental, psychological, cultural, and social, but which has been "cracked" within Western culture, by the same organization of knowledge, especially by the disjunction between science and philosophy and by disciplinary fragmentation.

In an attempt to circumvent the disciplinary division that is an obstacle to meta-knowledge, Morin observes that in the face of numerous models analyzed, there is one constant: the scientific movement of paradigm shift. Therefore, it is worth mentioning that an apparent constant of innovation cycles is the principle of uncertainty and the admission that disciplinary models are not permanent but contextualized and presumably fragile/volatile. This book thus proposes to understand the possibility of a model that addresses the depth of the interface between education and digital technologies and how it can be contextualized and constantly improved.

The SETA model seems to be a fruitful first step in composing an evaluative framework and a conceptual model. Harvesting the meaning of the word "SETA" in Portuguese (arrow), its acronym and name refer to the metaphor used by Latour to describe modernity as a natural progression of the unmerciless arrow of time. Also, the word "arrow" shelters the meaning of "target," bringing together the desire for localized actions that can improve the lives of targeted groups. The model's layered structure promotes the interaction with groups of actants to properly understand how the application of digital technology can be more meaningful, mainly (but not restricted) to education. There's still much work to be done, for example, collecting results and data based on its application in different contexts. However, the validation described in the last chapter brings an excellent first step for its appliance.

Applying and improving the model and its variables for future research is recommended. And be ready for the fact that maybe, technologies do not bring a new educational paradigm, despite presenting elements that could build a scenario for the dawn of a new reality. Nevertheless, it is prudent to avoid digital determinism and encourage the continued study of the conceptual categories elaborated and the reflection on the existence of other categorizations.

However, it is interesting to note that more than final considerations and future studies, this book ends (for now) with uncertainties. After exploring the scientific revolutions in the 20th century, Prigogine argues about the inexistence of certainty and how science raises more doubts than answers. This book proposes questions about the object studied as a first step in the palace of countless doubts that seem to be the scientific researcher's permanent home. In science, models and theories face actants and the strength or fragility of bonds established between these entities since the common issue is to learn which associations are more robust and which are weaker. They face the aggregation and disaggregation around the scientific fact giving rise to the movement of "translation," which, according to Latour, is the displacement between the domains of knowledge or, as the author himself puts it, between science and technology and society. Therefore, this work invites the reader to, instead of looking for answers, look for questions and perform the beautiful dance between fields of knowledge—which forms this extensive choreography called science.

Bibliography

ACCOTO, C. (2021). Il Mondo Ex Machina: cinque brevi Lezioni di Filosofia Dell'Automazione. Egea: Roma.

BAIRON, S. (2014). Tendências da Linguagem Científica Contemporânea em Expressividade Digital: uma problematização. Informática na Educação: teoria & prática, Porto Alegre.

BATESON, G. (1987). Steps to an Ecology of Mind: Collected Essays in Anthropology, Psychiatry, Evolution, and Epistemology. Jason Aronson Inc.

BONAMI, B., NEMORIN, S. (2020). Through three levels of abstraction: Towards an ecological framework for making sense of new technologies in education. https://doi.org/10.1007/s10639-020-10305-1

BONAMI, B. (2021). Dez Categorias que Expressam a Interface entre Tecnologia Digital, Comunicação e Educação: instrumento, empoderamento e rede de actantes. Tese de Doutorado, Escola de Comunicações e Artes, Universidade de São Paulo, São Paulo. doi:10.11606/T.27.2021.tde-24082021-210027. Recuperado em 2022-06-02, de www.teses.usp.br

BOURDIEU, P. (1986). Distinction (1st edition). Routledge.

BUCKINGHAM, D. (2010). Cultura Digital, Educação Midiática e o Lugar da Escolarização. Educação & Realidade, 35(3), Article 3. https://seer.ufrgs.br/educacaoerealidade/article/view/13077

CASTELLS, N. M., & ILLERA, J. L. R. (2018). Activity and learning contexts in educational transmedia. Digital Education Review, 0(33), 77–86. https://doi.org/10.1344/der.2018.33.77-86

DI FELICE, M. (2019). La cittadinanza digitale: La crisi dell'idea occidentale di democrazia e la partecipazione nelle reti digitali. Milan, Italy: Meltemi. 228 p. ISBN: 9788855190282

DIJCK, J. (2018). The Platform Society: Public Values in a Connective World. Oxford University Press.

DREYFUS, H. L. (1992). What Computers Still Can't Do: A Critique of Artificial Reason. MIT Press.

FLORIDI, L.(2014). The fourth revolution: how the infosphere is reshaping human reality. Oxford University Press UK.

GELL-MANN, M. (1994). The quark and the jaguar: Adventures in the simple and the complex.

HABER, S., & STORNETTA, W. S. (1991). How to time-stamp a digital document. Journal of Cryptology, 3(2), 99–111. https://doi.org/10.1007/BF00196791

HABERMAS, J. (1984). Theory of communicative action. Volume 1: Reason and the rationalisation of society. Beacon Press.

HEIDEGGER, M. (1977). The Question Concerning Technology, and Other Essays. Harper & Row.

HOBBES, T. (1968). Leviathan. Baltimore: Penguin Books.

JENKINS, H. (2006) Convergence Culture: Where Old and New Media Collide. New York: New York University Press.

JOHNSON, S. (2001). Cultura da interface: Como o computador transforma nossa maneira de criar e comunicar (1a edição). Zahar.

KANT, I. (2003). Critique of pure reason (M. Weigelt, Trans.). Penguin Classics.

KUHN, T. (1970). The Structure of Scientific Revolutions. Chicago: University of Chicago Press.

LARSON, E. (1989). They're Making a List. Washington Post. https://www.washingtonpost.com/archive/lifestyle/1989/07/27/the yre-making-a-list/dcbc7370-e3d0-489a-9848-3ebb7e6e4b79/

LATOUR, B. (1987). Science in Action: How to Follow Scientists and Engineers Through Society. Milton Keynes: Open University Press.

LATOUR, B. (1993). We Have Never Been Modern. Translated by Catherine Porter, Harvard University Press.

LATOUR, B. (1999). Pandora's hope: Essays on the reality of science studies. Cambridge, Mass: Harvard University Press.

LATOUR, B. (2005). Reassembling the social: An introduction to actor-network-theory. (ACLS Humanities E-Book.) Oxford: Oxford University Press.

LATOUR, B. (2007). Turning around Politics: A Note on Gerard de Vries' Paper. Social Studies of Science, 37(5), 811–820. http://www.jstor.org/stable/25474548

LATOUR, B. (2012). Biographie d'une enquête. À propos d'un livre sur les modes d'existence. Archives de Philosophie, 75, 549–566. https://doi.org/10.3917/aphi.754.0549

LATOUR, B. (2014). Give Me a Laboratory and I will Raise the World. In.: Parikshith S. STS Infrastructures, Platform for Experimental Collaborative Ethnography. Paris.

LEVY, P. (1997). Collective intelligence: Mankind's emerging world in cyberspace. New York: Plenum Trade.

MATURANA, H. R., & VARELA, F. J. (1987). The tree of knowledge: The biological roots of human understanding. New Science Library/Shambhala Publications.

MCLUHAN, M. (1966). Understanding media; the extensions of man. New York: Signet Books.

MEGA, T. B., ENDAH, B. R., & SUGI, H. (2017). Students abstraction in re-cognizing, building with and constructing a quadrilateral. Educational Research and Reviews, 12(7), 394–402. https://doi.org/10.5897/ERR2016.2977

MIEVILLE, C. (2010). The City & The City (Reprint edition). Del Rey.

MORIN, E. (1986). La Méthode (3eme tome): La Connaissance de la connaissance. Paris: Seuil.

MORIN, E. (2008). On complexity, Hampton Press, US.

NAESS, A. (2016). Ecology of Wisdom. Penguin Books: London, UK.

OLIVEIRA, M. M., & GIACOMAZZO, G. F. (2018.). Educação e cidadania: Perspectivas da literacia digital crítica. São Paulo, 43, 23.

PARKER, G. G., ALSTYNE, M. W. V., & CHOUDARY, S. P. (2016). Platform Revolution: How Networked Markets Are Transforming the Economy—And How to Make Them Work for You (1st edition). W. W. Norton & Company.

PAVLIK, J. V. (2015). Fueling a Third Paradigm of Education: The Pedagogical Implications of Digital, Social and Mobile Media. Contemporary Educational Technology, 6(2), Article 2. https://doi.org/10.30935/cedtech/6143

POTTER, J., & MCDOUGALL, J. (2017). Digital Media, Culture and Education: Theorising Third Space Literacies (pp. 61–81). Palgrave Macmillan UK. https://doi.org/10.1057/978-1-137-55315-7_4

PRIGOGINE, I., & STENGERS, I. (1997). The end of certainty: time, chaos, and the new laws of nature.

SANTAELLA, L. (2014). Hybrid Discursive Genres in the Hypermedia Era. In.: Bakhtiniana, São Paulo, 9 (2).

SELWYN, N. (2016). Is Technology Good for Education? (1a edição). Polity.

SERRES, M. (1995). The natural contract, Michigan University Press.

SIMONDON, G. (2005). L'Invention dans les techniques. Cours et conférences (Trace ï¿½crite edition). SEUIL.

SIMONDON, G. (2017). On the Mode of Existence of Technical Objects (C. Malaspina & J. Rogove, Trans.; 1st edition). Univ Of Minnesota Press.

SOURIAU, É. (2009). Les différents modes d'existence: Suivi de Du mode d'existence de l'œuvre à faire. Presses Universitaires de France. https://doi.org/10.3917/puf.souri.2009.01

SOE, S. O. (2018). Algorithmic detection of misinformation and disinformation: Gricean perspectives. Journal of Documentation, 74(2), 309–332. https://doi.org/10.1108/JD-05-2017-0075

THIRY-CHERQUES, H. R. (2006). Pierre Bourdieu: A teoria na prática. Revista de Administração Pública, 40(1), 27–53. https://doi.org/10.1590/S0034-76122006000100003

TURING, A. M. (1950). I.—Computing Machinery and Intelligence. Mind, LIX(236), 433–460. https://doi.org/10.1093/mind/LIX.236.433

UNGERER, L. M. (2016). Digital Curation as a Core Competency in Current Learning and Literacy: A Higher Education Perspective. The International Review of Research in Open and Distributed Learning, 17(5), Article 5. https://doi.org/10.19173/irrodl.v17i5.2566